FROM CARNEGIE TO CYBERSPACE

100 YEARS AT THE
CENTRAL ARKANSAS LIBRARY SYSTEM

SHIRLEY SCHUETTE AND NATHANIA SAWYER

www.butlercenter.org

The Butler Center for Arkansas Studies
Central Arkansas Library System
100 Rock Street
Little Rock, AR 72201

First edition: November 2010

ISBN-13: 978-1-935106-14-2
ISBN-10: 1-935106-14-7

PROJECT MANAGER: Rod Lorenzen
COPYEDITOR: Ali Welky
BOOK DESIGN: Wendell E. Hall
PAGE COMPOSITION: Shelly Culbertson

LIBRARY OF CONGRESS CATALOGING-IN-PUBLICATION DATA

Schuette, Shirley.
    From Carnegie to cyberspace: 100 years at the Central
Arkansas Library System / Shirley Schuette and Nathania
Sawyer. -- 1st ed.
        p. cm.
    Includes bibliographical references.
    ISBN-13: 978-1-935106-14-2 (alk. paper)
    ISBN-10: 1-935106-14-7 (alk. paper)
1. Central Arkansas Library System--History. 2. Public
libraries--Arkansas--History. I. Sawyer, Nathania K. II. Title.
    Z732.A7S38 2010
    027.4767'7--dc22

2010033846

This book is printed on archival-quality paper that meets requirements
of the American National Standard for Information Sciences, Permanence
of Paper, Printed Library Materials, ANSI Z39.48-1984.

Printed in Canada for customs

TABLE OF CONTENTS

Acknowledgements

First and foremost, I would like to thank Bobby Roberts for making this book possible and giving us the opportunity to be part of the 100th anniversary celebration.

Unless otherwise noted, photos and graphics in this book came from the Butler Center for Arkansas Studies archives and the Central Arkansas Library System's public relations department—many thanks go to Brian Robertson and Susan Hill Gelé for giving me access to their materials. Other photos are used courtesy of the *Arkansas Democrat-Gazette*, the Arkansas History Commission, the University of Illinois, and many individuals who shared their personal collections.

All of the credit for taking pages of words and a pile of graphics and making them into a beautiful book goes to Buster Hall and Shelly Culbertson, who did the design and typesetting for this book.

I would like to offer special thanks to the always amazing Encyclopedia of Arkansas History & Culture staff: Guy Lancaster for his brutally honest critiques, Mike Polston for his general knowledge of Arkansas history, Steve Teske for being my go-to guy for "can you help me find this obscure piece of information" questions, Michael Keckhaver for his insane abilities with a scanner, Anna Lancaster for keeping the ship afloat while I was on my in-office sabbatical, and Ali Welky for her thoughtful editing. I also would like to thank all of the CALS staff who agreed to be interviewed, shared their stories, offered their insights, dug through old files, filled in blanks, and provided encouragement throughout this project.

N. S.

I am grateful to all the people who assisted me with my research. Individuals with long institutional memory helped me sort out events and situations, including, but not limited to, Bob Razer, Valerie Thwing, Carolyn Cash, Bettye Kerns, and Bobby Roberts. Thanks also to Lee Razer, who tracked down numerous resources for me through Interlibrary Loan, and to the branch managers who gave me important insights into how the library functions in their communities.

My research benefited greatly from being on the "cyberspace" end of this continuum. Thanks to the Internet, I was able to locate critical archival collections, academic works, and government reports, as well as make contact with other library historians—librarians and archivists that they are, they responded graciously and shared resources generously.

S. S.

INTRODUCTION

"That public library is never a complete success, in which is not present in the officers a spirit of courtesy toward readers, of sympathy, of cheerfulness, of patience, even of helpfulness… Let [your library] always be a bright and winsome place, hospitable to all orderly people; a place where even those ill-informed about books will not be made embarrassed, but encouraged."[1]

MOSES COIT TYLER, 1884

The Central Arkansas Library System (CALS) exemplifies the "bright and winsome place" that historian Moses Coit Tyler envisioned in his 1884 essay. CALS began in 1910 as the Little Rock Public Library, which was housed in a classically designed building funded by the Carnegie Foundation. Early patrons, such as author Dee Brown, were drawn to it as the place that opened up the world of books to them. One hundred years later, the library system continues its commitment to be a beacon in the community and to prepare patrons of all ages to be a part of the larger world through providing free access to books, art, audio/visual materials, public programming, and much more.

Tyler's challenge to libraries came at a time when most libraries were available only to scholars or to people of wealth; only a few hundred "public" libraries existed in the entire country, and none were located in Arkansas.

Writing at about the same time, Chinese missionary and scholar W. A. P. Martin noted that the Chinese written character usually translated as "library" literally meant "a place to hide books."[2] Many early libraries operated in just that fashion; access was only for certain groups of people, hours were limited, and the circulation of books was not allowed. Librarians focused more on building their collections and protecting them than they did on encouraging people to read the books.

This situation changed as the public library movement spread across the country—in part because the public wanted libraries and in part because community leaders saw in the public library a way to shape and mold the rising urban and industrial populations.

In Little Rock, the library movement took hold during the last quarter of the nineteenth century, with the founding of mercantile and subscription libraries, and at the beginning of the twentieth century, with a campaign for a free public library.

Many early libraries operated on a subscription basis; if you paid an enrollment fee and/or a monthly service fee, you could check out books. Well-to-do individuals often accumulated large personal libraries that they sometimes made available to other people to use, but these collections required individuals to have a connection with the owners in order to gain access. Another form of limited-access library consisted of collections gathered by organizations for their members' use—again with limited access to the general public.

"Free," of course, is a misnomer because libraries are never free. The question from the beginning of the movement focused on who would pay for the overhead and maintenance to sustain the library.

Philanthropist Andrew Carnegie believed that the only way to provide a free-access library was to have it funded by a government or quasi-governmental organization. When he began providing grants to build public libraries, he required applicant communities to make a commitment to provide an annual budget equal to at least ten percent of the grant amount. In most cases, city governments made this commitment, although many of them struggled to maintain that level of funding.

Until 1940, most of the capital and operational funding for libraries in Arkansas came from city budgets, through regular city income streams. Some state aid became available in 1937 for establishing county libraries, but continuing operational funds came only from county budgets, again through the regular budgeting process and regular income streams. A major portion of the library director's efforts during these years went to overcoming the political resistance to providing adequate funding.

Writing in the June 2, 1935, issue of the *Arkansas Democrat*, William Johnson challenged the status quo for libraries in Arkansas, regarding both funding and commitment. At the time, only 15 percent of Arkansans had access to libraries, compared to 98 percent of Californians. Even other Southern states had better records than Arkansas: Alabama, 68 percent; Georgia, 71 percent; Louisiana, 62 percent; and Mississippi, 69 percent. Johnson suggested that, in addition to other states having more money, they had a stronger commitment to education as a road to prosperity.

Arkansas's continued reliance on the cotton economy produced a concerted resistance to education that might draw the labor supply away from the plantations. After talking about the substantial home libraries of members of the planter class, Johnson said: "Public libraries must take [the] place [of home libraries], if the South is to share fully in the progress and prosperity of the nation. For all advancement, and all power, come of knowledge and of ideas. A library is not just a house full of books—it is a treasury of information and thought. As such, it is a mental and spiritual power plant, energizing life, and making it more amply richly effective."[3]

Dr. Bessie Boehm Moore, whose leadership role in the library field had begun about the time that Johnson was writing, spoke in 1975 of the challenges faced by libraries in fulfilling this role. "In this interdependent society," she said, "few problems can be isolated and must be considered in relation to other problems and issues. Library problems are a good example. They are tied up with problems relating to education, problems of taxation at all levels, matters of policy, and attitudes toward institutions in general, all of which affect libraries."[4]

The financial history of CALS traces the development of funding sources from the original Carnegie grant and private donations through the developments of the last seventy years: *ad valorem* taxes, with funds dedicated to the library; state grants funded by legislative appropriations; federal grants for library construction and development; and the passage in 1992 of Amendment 3, which not only made funding more stable but also has provided for significant growth and expansion.

Regardless of the amount of available funding, the prime directive of CALS has stayed the same: to provide public service to the citizens of central Arkansas. Mary Maud Pugsley stated that the library's goal was the "building up [of] a reading public...That a higher standard of citizenship and a better civic life may grow up among us, this is our aim and this will be our justification."[5] Successive library directors and staff members continued to emphasize public service as the focus of their efforts.

Such service takes the form not just of making a collection of books and other information sources available at the library, but of reaching out into the community through public programming. As library historian Phyllis Dain wrote in her history of the New York Public Library, a city's library functions as "a repository of its records, a disseminator of information, and a medium of education and recreation."[6] With few exceptions, fulfilling this function, providing this service to the people, has remained the driving force for the leadership, the staff, and the supporters of the Central Arkansas Library System. The esteem in which the library has been held by community members throughout its history speaks of the success of these dedicated individuals and groups.

Historian Robert Leigh stated, "The community's library stands for much that is cherished in our tradition of equal educational opportunity and freedom of thought and communication. It takes its place along with the courthouse, the school, the church, and the town hall as an integral part of the American scene."[7]

From its beginning, the Little Rock Public Library fit well with Leigh's description of the library as one of the monumental buildings in a community. One hundred years later, CALS provides not one, but many separate library branches and buildings to serve the needs of the expanding population. As the system has expanded, the goal remains for each new location to be a beacon in the community.

While Leigh described the public library in America as the "traditional custodian of the printed word,"[8] in the succeeding sixty years, the public library's task has expanded substantially beyond the written word. Dr. Bessie Boehm Moore, in her 1975 speech in Louisiana, spoke of the important larger concept of libraries as custodians of information: "We cannot afford to do less than to treat information as a national resource."[9]

The following history of the Central Arkansas Library System places the story of the organization in the context of history of the city of Little Rock and the state of Arkansas. It tells the story of how one small library that served a city with a population of less than 50,000 grew into a major system that serves nearly 350,000 people in two counties, and how that system also provides statewide leadership in the library community.

---

1 Moses Coit Tyler, "The Historic Evolution of the Free Public Library in America and Its True Function in the Community," *Library Journal* (March 1884), in *Contributions to American Library History*, ed. Thelma Eaton (Champaign: The Illini Union Book Store, 1961).

2 W. N. Chattin Carlton, "College Libraries in the Mid-Nineteenth Century," *Library Journal* (November 1907), 479–86, in *Contributions to American Library History*, ed. Thelma Eaton (Champaign: The Illini Union Book Store, 1961)

3 *Arkansas Democrat*, June 2, 1935.

4 Moore delivered the Louisiana State University Library Distinguished Lecture in 1975. Full text of the lecture is available in George and Mildred Fersh, *Bessie Moore, A Biography* (Little Rock: August House, 1986).

5 Report dated November 11, 1912.

6 Phyllis Dain, *The New York Public Library: A History of Its Founding and Early Years* (New York: The New York Public Library, Astor, Lenox, and Tilden Foundations, 1972), xvi.

7 Robert D. Leigh, *The Public Library in the United States*. New York: Columbia University Press, 1950.

8 Leigh, *Public Library*, 1950.

9 Fersh, *Bessie Moore*.

chapter one

THE EARLY DEVELOPMENT OF LIBRARIES

"In many towns, and in every city, they have publick [*sic*] libraries. Not a tradesman but will find time to read. He acquires knowledge imperceptibly. He is amused with voyages and travels, and becomes acquainted with the geography, customs, and commerce of tother [*sic*] countries. He reads political disquisitions, and learns the great outlines of his rights as a man and as a citizen."[1]

A FOREIGN VISITOR AT THE TIME OF THE AMERICAN REVOLUTION

Libraries in America developed in a unique manner, largely because of the great influx of immigrants of various social classes. These immigrants included many bookish people who had left their homelands in part because of the influence of ideas.[2] Even poorer families might have two or three precious books among their possessions. Many of these people emphasized education in their families and wanted to provide their children opportunities to "better themselves."

Before the development of public libraries, working-class people had limited options for accessing books. Many well-to-do men had private libraries—some of which contained thousands of volumes—that they would share with others. However, the vast majority of the working class did not have access to these private libraries.

Early proponents of accessible libraries worked to provide books through institutions. At the beginning of the eighteenth century, Rev. John Bray placed libraries in thirty-nine Anglican parishes throughout the colonies. When John Harvard died in 1638, he left his library to a college being established by the Colony of Massachusetts, forming the basis for the institution that was subsequently named for him. His gift created the first of many such academic libraries in America.[3]

Throughout the colonial period, reading rooms, bookstores, and libraries of various kinds responded to the reading interests of a broad spectrum of the population. Coffee houses became de facto communication centers where people could read newspapers from all over the colonies, in addition to the occasional book[4]—not unlike the coffee houses and bookstores today that offer access to a variety of printed material and wireless access to the Internet.

Types of Early "Public" Libraries

Libraries that organized to serve a wider audience than the academic and private libraries fall into three broad headings: social libraries, circulating libraries, and mercantile or mechanics libraries. At least one library of each of these types existed in Little Rock during the nineteenth century.

Social libraries were established by associations or sometimes corporations that existed to make book collections available to members. Some associations operated on a subscription basis in which members paid a yearly or monthly fee, and some were based on shares of stock in which members bought a share in the organization. The first and best-known of these, the Library Company of Philadelphia, was founded in 1731 by Benjamin Franklin and other members of the Junto, a literary organization. This type of library was sometimes referred to as "public" because it was open to anyone who could afford to join or buy in.

Circulating libraries, common in Eastern cities as early as the 1820s and 1830s, sometimes were located in print shops, post offices, clothing stores, general stores, or other locations where people tended to gather. The financial structure for these libraries varied—sometimes including a subscription fee, a charge for renting books, or a combination of both. The characteristics of circulating libraries presented a change from the earlier, more scholarly libraries, setting the stage for people's expectations of public libraries as they began to develop. These expectations included having extended hours so that patrons could read current newspapers and magazines; providing service to both men and women; offering what the people wanted, not just what the intellectuals thought people should read; and providing on-site reading rooms as well as circulation privileges.[5]

Businesses or organizations of workers started mercantile and mechanics libraries to provide reading material that would help the workmen or clerks improve their situation. Their activities often went beyond having a book collection and included public lectures or musical events. There was usually a fee associated with these libraries, but they were also often supported by employers.

Although these libraries often were referred to as public libraries, only those who could afford the fees or who were part of a certain group of people had access to them. They were not equally available to everyone in the community, nor were they supported by public funds, and thus not genuinely public.

Development of the Public Library

The public library as we know it today began to develop in the mid-nineteenth century. An 1876 report by the United States Department of Education defined a public library as one that "is established by state laws, is supported by local taxation or voluntary gifts, is managed as a public trust, and every citizen of the city or town which maintains it has an equal share in its privileges of reference and circulation."[6] Gradually, such libraries came to be accepted as a public responsibility in the same way that education became a public responsibility and an appropriate use of tax money.

The Boston Public Library, which opened in 1854, generally gets credit for being the first true public library in the United States. However, the publicly supported town library of Peterborough, New Hampshire, was more than twenty years old when Boston's library opened. Formed in 1833 with a budget of $60 a year, the Peterborough Town Library still operates today.

Between 1848 and 1875, 188 public libraries were established in the United States. By 1896, the number had grown to 971 public libraries that had at least 1,000 books, as well as many more with smaller collections. Especially in the northern and eastern parts of the country, the public library became an expected sight in towns and cities of all sizes. This expectation expanded into other parts of the country and played a role in the growth of libraries in the South.

The Growth of the Library Movement

A major factor in the spread of public libraries involved the improved printing processes that made the mass production of books and other reading material possible. With the resulting greater availability of books, the size of the reading public also grew. This growth continued during the years of increased industrialization, as workers actually had more leisure time. The role of the librarian, which had been largely custodial, shifted toward more involvement in guiding the reading choices of library patrons.[7]

Supporters of public libraries increasingly looked to libraries as a means to provide an educated labor force, as well as an electorate better prepared for voting. Library historian Sidney Ditzion identified the role libraries played in supporting democracy: they took up "the educational process where the schools left off and by conducting a people's university, a wholesome capable citizenry would be fully schooled in the conduct of a democratic life."[8]

Libraries also were viewed as a tool to help new immigrants learn the language and begin to assimilate into the American culture.[9] This role raised the question of whether to provide books in immigrants' native languages. Some people resisted this idea on the basis that it would discourage the immigrants from learning English and thus hamper assimilation.

Librarians, however, generally favored having books in the appropriate languages. They maintained that the library itself provided an Americanizing influence, but it would not be useful if it did not provide reading material in the language the immigrant understood. The older immigrants were unlikely to be fully Americanized, but it was possible to provide books in their language that promoted American history and civic life, thus effecting their Americanization. Younger people, especially the children, would learn English quickly and need books in English.[10]

Another factor among the social and intellectual conditions that supported library growth centered on the call for "progress" and "self-improvement." The growth of public libraries followed closely the growth of free public education and the proliferation of programs that promoted adult education, such as lyceums. Eventually, the public library was seen as a critical component of a good public education and therefore an appropriate use for public funds. Library supporters argued that the government was committed to providing a free education for its youth up until "the time when it could be most profitably utilized."[11] The schools turned out literate, habitual readers who needed to continue their education in preparation for work and worthy citizenship. Without the public library, these individuals did not have reading material available.

The role of women's clubs in the library movement cannot be overstated. "The real function of the women's organizations in the public library movement was…to crusade in small towns which were tardy in supporting a library, to stir up interest in slow states by lobbying for legislation, and to carry the movement to recently settled or educationally backward parts of the country. The last decade of the nineteenth century found women's organizations feverishly campaigning for free libraries in the Midwest and West and, at the very end of the century, trying to stir up interest in the South."[12] Little Rock was one such location.

1 James Lyman Whitney, "Incidents in the History of the Boston Public Library," American Library Association, *Conference of Librarians, Boston and Magnolia, Mass.* (June 16–20, 1902), in *Contributions to American Library History*, ed. Thelma Eaton (Champaign: The Illini Union Book Store, 1961), 181.

2 Moses Coit Tyler, "The Historic Evolution of the Free Public Library in America and Its True Function in the Community," *Library Journal* (March 1884), in *Contributions to American Library History*, ed. Thelma Eaton (Champaign: The Illini Union Book Store, 1961).

3 Jesse H. Shera, *Foundations of the Public Library: The Origins of the Public Library Movement in New England 1629–1855.* Hamden, CT: The Shoe String Press, 1974 (originally published by University of Chicago Press, 1947).

4 David Kaser, *A Book for Sixpence: The Circulating Library in America* (Pittsburgh, PA: Beta Phi Mu, 1980).

5 Kaser, *Book for Sixpence.*

6 United States Bureau of Education; University of Wisconsin Digital Collections Center. *Public Libraries in the United States of America; Their History, Condition, and Management. Special report, Department of the Interior, Bureau of Education. Part I.* Washington: Government Printing Office, 1876, online at http://digital.library.wisc.edu/1711.dl/History. PublicLibs. (accessed May 14, 2009).

7 Matthew Battles, *Library: An Unquiet History* (New York: W. W. Norton & Co., 2003), 120.

8 Sidney Herbert Ditzion, *Arsenals of a Democratic Culture: A Social History of the American Public Library Movement in New England and the Middle States from 1850 to 1900.* (Chicago: American Library Association, 1947), 74.

9 Phyllis Dain, *The New York Public Library: A History of Its Founding and Early Years* (New York: The New York Public Library, Astor, Lenox, and Tilden Foundations, 1972)

10 Ditzion, *Arsenals of a Democratic Culture*, 75; Arthur E. Bostwick, *The American Public Library* (New York: D. Appleton and Company, 1910), 51.

11 Ditzion, *Arsenals of a Democratic Culture.*

12 Ditzion, *Arsenals of a Democratic Culture*, 83

chapter two

THE BIRTH OF THE LITTLE ROCK PUBLIC LIBRARY

"The women of the city are not going to rest until they have secured this public library."

FLORENCE COTNAM, 1906

Although Little Rock did not succeed in getting a true public library until 1910, individuals and groups made several attempts at establishing some form of library for the fledgling community. One of the earliest attempts took place a full decade before Arkansas became a state.

Woodruff Circulating Library

William Woodruff, founder of the *Arkansas Gazette*, brought the concept of the circulating library to Arkansas from Brooklyn. At least one circulating library had existed there when he worked as an apprentice to printer and newspaperman Alden Spooner.[1] Woodruff published his newspaper in Little Rock beginning in 1821 (two years after founding the paper at Arkansas Post) when Little Rock was little more than a village with a population of fewer than 500 people. Like many printers back East, Woodruff sold books, stationery, and other goods that brought customers to his shop. He tried to establish a circulating library in November 1826—apparently with limited success.

Woodruff's second attempt at creating a circulating library occurred in 1843, several years after he had sold the *Arkansas Gazette*. For an annual membership of $2, patrons could obtain books and keep them for up to two weeks. During the Civil War, Little Rock fell to the Union troops on September 10, 1863, and Woodruff stored the books in the home of his eldest son. His attempt to protect

William Woodruff, circa 1830.
From the collections of the Arkansas History Commission.

the books proved futile. When a fire broke out in a nearby building, Woodruff's son moved the books into the street for safety, where passing Union soldiers helped themselves to the books.

Woodruff's daughter Jane wrote a description of the library in November 1919 for the centennial edition of the *Arkansas Gazette*. It is possible that this description contains a bit of hyperbole, perhaps more accurately describing Woodruff's personal library rather than what he offered for public distribution: "All of the best histories, ancient and modern, Irving's, Scott's, Dickens', in fact all standard novels, with travels and scientific works, were neatly shelved and accessible to all who wished to read them. There was nothing trashy. My father's taste was for the best literature and he encouraged us to read it."[2]

David Kaser lists Woodruff's library in his book *A Book for Sixpence: The Circulating Library in America*, which discusses circulating libraries in the nineteenth century. He credits American workers' increased leisure reading and the success of the novel in the popularity of circulating libraries; they provided less-serious, less-scholarly reading material than other libraries.

During the period between Woodruff's attempts to establish a library, the Little Rock Debating Society assembled a library to support its programs. In October 1834, members of the society decided to open the library to anyone who wanted to use it, seeing this move as a first step in establishing a public library in Little Rock.[3]

One other pre–Civil War library in Little Rock deserves mention. Well-known Little Rock lawyer Albert Pike had an extensive personal library and occasionally lent books from it. At one point, he put an ad in the newspaper saying that several books were unaccounted for and asking for their return.

Mercantile/Marquand/YMCA Library

The Mercantile Library, organized on November 15, 1867, was open to young men in the business and retail community of Little Rock. It was established "for the purpose of collecting a library and cabinet, establishing a reading room, and organizing a system of instruction, by lectures, classes, and such other means of mutual improvement as may be found advantageous."[4]

The library depended on donations both for books and operating funds. In June 1870, the organizers appealed to the community to help add to its collection and also to support it financially. The library—located in a room next to the office of R. L. Goodrich, clerk of the Federal Court—was situated at the southeast corner of Markham and Rock streets and was open on Saturdays from 2:00 to 5:00 p.m.[5] It later moved to the northeast corner of Main and 4th streets, and then to a room over Wolf & Bros. Dry Goods Store on Main between 4th and 5th streets.

In its annual report for 1870, the operators of the Mercantile Library reported that it owned 1,087 volumes, and that they "were not in debt to anyone." By June 1871, the hours of service had expanded; the library was open from 4:00 to 6:00 p.m. every day for checking out books and at other times for use of the reading room. The organizers hoped the library's usage might grow enough for the library to warrant its own building.

From Carnegie to Cyberspace: 100 Years at the Central Arkansas Library System

Y. M. C. A. Little Rock, Ark.

In 1904, the YMCA built this building, designed by Charles Thompson.

In addition to operating the reading room, the Mercantile Library Association sponsored lectures—both to promote education and to raise funds for the library. Eventually, the efforts going into the lecture events overshadowed the book services. The fortunes of the Mercantile Library rose and fell throughout the 1870s and early 1880s.

The Marquand Library was established through a gift from Henry G. Marquand, president of the St. Louis and Iron Mountain Railroad, who wanted to provide a library for railroad employees. Rather than duplicate services, the organizers of the Marquand Library and the Mercantile Library merged their resources, with the new library housed at the headquarters of the railroad company at the corner of Cross and Markham streets. The collection was later housed in the Young Men's Christian Association (YMCA) building and came to be called the YMCA Library.

The library continued to be available as part of the YMCA programs, with privileges also available to women, for a fee of $1 per year. New books were added to the collection as late as 1898. The 1908 Little Rock City Directory listed the YMCA at 5th and Scott streets[6] as being home of a circulating library containing 3,000 books.

Available records do not show exactly when the YMCA Library closed, but many years later, the remains of the collection were accessioned by the Little Rock Public Library.

Woman's Cooperative Association Library

When the Woman's Cooperative Association (WCA) organized and incorporated in 1895, its founders' stated goals were "to found and maintain a library, encourage intellectual, social, moral and physical culture, and to promote philanthropy."[7]

The association's goal of starting a library came to fruition in 1897 under the leadership of association president Adolphine Krause Fletcher[8] and chairperson of the library department Emily Blakeslee Roots. In early February, they hosted a book reception at the home of former governor James P. Eagle and his wife, asking those attending to bring books to contribute to their library. They asked for "standard works by authors old and new and first class magazines. Something that you wish your son, daughter or friend to read." More than 100 people attended and contributed 300 books, with "very few duplicates and not one unworthy a place on the shelves of any home."[9]

The Arsenal Building, birthplace of General Douglas MacArthur, for whom MacArthur Park is named.

Their call for book donations expressed their goal for the library: "The present war cry is, Books! Books! and plenty of them, so they are good literature by good authors that will inspire noble thoughts in the minds of the sons and daughters of Little Rock." While they no doubt recognized the value of reading as entertainment, their goal was education and character building.

The library was located on the second floor of the Arsenal Building in City Park (modern-day MacArthur Park). At the WCA's meeting on March 26, 1897, they assembled a committee of five women—all of whom with experience teaching in the public schools—to transform the collected books into an accessible library. Dr. Ida Jo Brooks served as chairperson of the committee. Following their April 7 meeting, they announced, "The new library under the auspices of the Woman's Co-Operative Association will be open for reading and the registration of pupils who wish to become members or donate books every evening this week from 4 to 5 o'clock, in the library rooms in the city park."[10]

Association members paid a fee of two dollars per year, which gave them unlimited access to the library. Non-association members could become library members by paying a fee of one dollar per year for adults and 25 cents a year for juveniles.[11] The association's librarian, who was paid a modest monthly stipend, oversaw the library operations and reported to the group at the first regular meeting of the month on the condition and business matters of the library. Other women's organizations in the city supported the work of the library; for example, the Educational Aid Society, whose main goal was to provide assistance to young women in pursuing their education, provided forty memberships to children who could not pay the annual dues.

Early Attempts at Establishing a Library
for the African-American Community

Some members of Little Rock's African-American community took steps early on to provide for their educational needs. In 1890, a group met in Little Rock with the intention of establishing a library.[12] In 1898, women of the Little Rock branch of the Colored Woman's Federated Clubs, who according to D. B. Gaines were "the most progressive and intelligent women of the city," made plans for a reading room for their community.[13]

For African Americans in the South, the struggle was not just with a lack of resources, but with a culture that often made it dangerous to be an educated black person. Those who recognized the need—and many in the community did— also recognized the obstacles to bringing about even limited library service to the black community.

Within the next decade, a few examples of libraries or library branches existed in the black communities of Southern cities. An independent public library for African Americans opened in Charlotte, North Carolina, in 1903, the same year that the Memphis Public Library entered into a contract with LeMoyne College (a black school founded in 1870) to open its library to the black community. The first branch library for African Americans opened in 1904 in Galveston, Texas, followed the next year by one in Louisville, Kentucky. The Louisville library became very well known and was the first organization to provide formal training for black librarians.

Building Support for a Public Library

The formation of the Arkansas Federation of Women's Clubs (AFWC) in 1897 reinforced the effort to create public libraries. The WCA was a charter member of the AFWC. Both the new statewide organization and many local organizations sought to establish libraries that "would not be for the use or benefit of club women only, but for all, without distinction of class." These might be brick-and-mortar libraries in cities or towns, or they might be traveling libraries that could be taken into "every city, town, village or community which asks for them." The women were prepared to do what it took to convince the people of the need, and to petition and persuade the governor or the legislature to make it happen.[14]

Even as the WCA worked to establish its library, the members realized that a free public library was needed. The other organizations that supported reading rooms and limited libraries staffed by volunteers also knew that such efforts could not adequately meet the needs of the reading public in the city. So, the WCA set out to establish a library that would meet growing needs.

Their first challenge was to convince the public and the politicians of the need; the second challenge was to meet all the requirements and find the resources to make the public library a reality. The timing of their efforts coincided with Andrew Carnegie's philanthropic efforts to build libraries in American cities and towns.

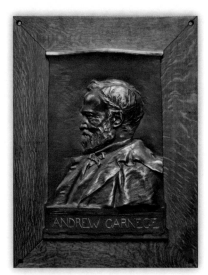

"If it is right that schools should be maintained by the whole community for the well-being of the whole, it is right also that libraries should be so maintained."

ANDREW CARNEGIE, 1904

The Little Rock Public Library received this plaque from the Carnegie Foundation to acknowledge Andrew Carnegie's funding of the library building.

The first American public library funded by Andrew Carnegie was built in Braddock, Pennsylvania, in 1889. By the end of the century, he had underwritten the construction of libraries in seventeen states, and his philanthropy had become widely known.[15] News about the available funding served as the catalyst for many communities to move forward in establishing public libraries.

The Library as a Public Trust

Andrew Carnegie, a Scotch-Irish industrialist who worked his way up from a factory worker as a child to one of the richest men in America, is best known as a steel magnate and philanthropist. When he retired from business in 1901, he set out in earnest to distribute his immense wealth to causes he supported. By the time of his death in 1919, Carnegie had distributed approximately $350 million to support his interests, including funding library construction and providing church organs to local communities.

Carnegie believed that the wealthy should live moderately, provide for their families, and then use the surplus to give to the community. He saw the wealthy as trustees with responsibility to manage their wealth, and they were better able to do this than the community itself. The wealthy should help the poor but not do everything for them; just giving to people and groups without expecting some measure of responsibility on their part was not helpful.[16]

Carnegie saw America as a meritocracy in which anyone with intelligence and determination could be successful; education, especially as libraries facilitated it, aided in that process. He attributed his success and his commitment to libraries to a man who opened his private collection to young working-class men on Sunday afternoons. He also saw libraries as important to immigrants, providing them with a means to learn more about America and to become more socialized into American beliefs and ways. "There was no use to which money could be applied so productive of good to boys and girls who have good within them and ability and ambition to develop it, as the founding of a public library in a community....In a public library men could at least share cultural opportunities on a basis of equality."[17]

To qualify for Carnegie library funds, which averaged $2 per capita based on the population numbers from the most recent census, a local community was required to:

- Demonstrate the need for a public library
- Provide the building site
- Commit to support the library by providing an annual operating budget equal to ten percent of the cost of the library's construction grants.

The majority of the work in administering library grants fell to Carnegie's secretary, James Bertram. Carnegie, and especially Bertram, developed a structured process for dealing with requests for library grants and, by 1908, had stringent requirements that had to be met. The stronger regulations, which included a requirement that building plans be approved, were put in place to ensure more careful planning and eliminate overruns on building and furnishing costs. Once the rules were in place, Bertram and Carnegie rarely made an exception to them. As they refined the grant-making process, they also brought about significant changes in library design and in how libraries functioned.

Carnegie was adamant that cities provide ten percent of the grant amount yearly for maintenance of the library and its programs rather than a gift or endowment fund. Carnegie emphasized the responsibility of the town government to provide for and care for the library—libraries were established through philanthropy, but once they were in existence, they were a public trust.[18]

Carnegie wrote, "I do not think that the community which is not willing to maintain a Library had better possess it. It is only the feeling that the Library belongs to every citizen richest and poorest alike, that gives it a soul, as it were. The Library Buildings which I am giving are the property of all the members of the community which maintain them."[19]

Securing Carnegie Funding for the Little Rock Public Library

The first inquiry to Andrew Carnegie from Little Rock came through the schools. The board of directors that oversaw the city schools appointed a library committee, with J. W. Biedelman as chairman. This committee corresponded with the Carnegie organization asking for advice on how to proceed and seeking funding for a building and an adequate collection.

A letter to the Carnegie organization dated November 9, 1900, described the great need for a library for the schoolchildren and the efforts even the children were making to meet this need: "Our School Children gave an entertainment for the purpose of raising Funds for a library and we have five hundred dollars on deposit now. This Board I know will furnish a location and will provide a librarian if demanded but cannot with the limited means at our hands either build a suitable building or purchase the needed books; what we need particularly is a reference collection of books, where all could have free access."

Bertram's terse response directed this committee to the city for help; he asked what the city would do to furnish a site and maintain a free public library. Without that commitment, Carnegie would not consider any request for help.

The first step in making free public libraries available in Arkansas occurred in 1901 when the state passed its first library law, which permitted some cities to maintain a library if it was established with private funds.[20] This law spurred many of the women's organizations to begin collecting books or funds to support libraries; often, the women themselves staffed a reading room as volunteer librarians.

The next inquiry to Carnegie came in 1902 from Margaret Braddock, wife of John Braddock, the president of Braddock Land and Granite Company. Braddock hoped to sway Carnegie with a promise that the library would be built of the "magnificent grey granite" that was available within two miles of the city. Because the granite was available locally, she said, a building that would cost $150,000 in the North and East could be built in Little Rock for $50,000.

The Braddocks had come to the area three years prior and were "astonished to find so many cultured people without what [people] in the North and East consider an *absolute necessity*, a Public Library." The only library at the time, Mrs. Braddock said, was "a library of 2,000 volumes in a little room in the old Arsenal building in the City Park," supported by a few women who "pay a lady $10 per month to keep the room open from 3 to 5 p.m. each day."

When Mrs. Braddock took the matter up with the city, she discovered a road-block; the Little Rock City Council could not levy money to support a library without passage of a state law authorizing it to do so. Carnegie was adamant that he would not work with private libraries but only with public libraries. Nothing more could be done until the legislature took up the matter and until the city was ready to take on the obligation.

Fred W. Allsopp, then business manager at the *Arkansas Gazette*, wrote to Andrew Carnegie in May 1904. He spoke of the earlier requests not being successful "on account of the fact that our people are averse to creating public debts, because of past bitter experiences, and as our taxes are already high." His purpose in writing was to ask if there was any way Carnegie would consider even a small donation despite the lack of city cooperation. The answer, of course, was no.

In July 1905, J. N. Heiskell, editor of the *Arkansas Gazette*, wrote to Carnegie pleading Little Rock's case with the written support of Mayor W. R. Lenon. In response to the question about whether Arkansas had a law allowing a library tax, Heiskell pointed out that, although there was a constitutional limit on the amount a city could impose in taxes, cities were free to allocate any portion of their taxes to a public library.

May Voss, president of the WCA, wrote several letters dated October through December 1905.[21] Voss was working to bring all of the pieces together so that Little Rock would meet the requirements for a grant. This included providing a copy of the April 13, 1903, Arkansas state law empowering "cities of the first and second class" to levy taxes up to ¼ mill for the purpose of supporting a library, as long as their total taxes did not exceed five mills.[22]

All of this correspondence and the efforts behind it led up to the plan to put a request for support of a public library on the agenda for the city council in January 1906. This included bringing the subject before the people to build community support.

On January 23, a delegation of sixty women representing organizations in the city appeared before the city council asking for its commitment to providing land for a library and funding its maintenance and operations in accordance with the requirements of the Carnegie grants. The communication presented to the council was signed by representatives of the Cosmopolitan Club, Free Kindergarten Library, Edelweiss Club, Provident Relief Association, Aesthetic Club, Woman's Christian Temperance Union, Novel Book Club, Young Men's Christian Association Auxiliary, Business Woman's Club, Musical Coterie, Tuesday Musical Club, Educational Aid Association, Mothers' Club, Woman's Cooperative Association, Self-Culture Club, and Bay View Club.

They asked that the council appoint a committee made up of the mayor and the city attorney to negotiate with Andrew Carnegie for a grant to build a free public library. Their request also included the donation of land in City Park for the building pending approval of the grant, and that a ¼ mill tax be levied annually to support the library, not to exceed $5,000/year.[23]

Voss, speaking as chairman of the delegation, said, "We are very much in earnest in this matter, and we hope the Council will not let this opportunity pass to secure a library, a movement in the interest of every citizen of the city." Frances M. Hanger, Georgia Jones, Bernie Babcock, Clara Martin, and Florence Cotnam also spoke to the question. Cotnam succinctly expressed the position of the group when she said that they believed the city was well able to spend the funds required, and that the women "would not rest" until the library became a reality.[24]

Discussion ensued about the location of the library, with some suggesting that the City Park site might not be feasible. Although the question of location remained to be answered, the resolutions passed unanimously. Nevertheless, much remained to be done, and it would be another four years before the library opened.

After several exchanges about the required paperwork, Bertram wrote on March 24, 1906, that Carnegie had approved a grant of $50,000, still dependent on a clear resolution of the city council committing the city to the $5,000 per year appropriation.

Discussions continued throughout 1906 on what needed to be done to meet Carnegie's requirements without placing an undue burden on the city budget and to resolve the question of location. Nearly two years would pass between the meeting at which the city council first gave approval to the women's proposal and when the question of location was finally settled.

One of the committee members, Georgia Jackson Jones, enlisted the help of Samuel Reyburn to solve the location problem. Initial discussions centered on using space in City Park. However, as the members understood it, Carnegie required that ownership of the building would revert to him if a city failed to keep its commitment to maintaining a library.[25] Ceding ownership was not an option for a building located in City Park. Others thought a location closer to the business district would be better.

As president of Union Trust Company, Reyburn was aware of the project and had been approached by real estate owners. However, he might not have taken an active part had his former history teacher not approached him about it. Reyburn said, "'Miss Georgia,' as I called her, was logical and forceful, if not tactful. To her the bank president was still her 8th grade pupil. On proving her points that Little Rock had been pretty good to me and I had done nothing for it, she persuaded, or bullied, me into taking up the cause."[26]

Efforts up to that point had centered on asking Carnegie for $50,000. This figure may have come from Braddock's statement that a granite building could be built for that amount. Reyburn and others he enlisted to help thought the grant request should be for at least $100,000, which would increase the commitment Carnegie required for ongoing support to $10,000 a year.

Throughout late 1905 and early 1906, Heiskell published editorials in the *Gazette* promoting a free public library in Little Rock. On January 11, 1906, he spoke to the Woman's Cooperative Association on the subject "Does Little Rock Need a Public Library?" According to Heiskell, the people of the city needed a public library because a library:

- Would be a place where we could get information

- Would furnish to children books to amuse them and to develop their constructive and artistic faculties

- May be made to shed light on current events

- Serves as a rallying point for literary, artistic, scientific, and other clubs and societies

- Is a reservoir of city and state history

- Would furnish endless amusement and diversion

- Would supply useful and valuable information to trades and professions

- Would increase our population

- Would catch and hold the publications that are given to libraries free, but may be lost if not secured when published

- Is the most valuable adjunct of the schools

On November 16, 1906, a group of businessmen involved with the committee met with Mayor Lenon. They argued that a $100,000 building would meet Little Rock's needs much more effectively in the long term than the $50,000 building discussed earlier. The committee brought a proposal on how the city could commit to the required $10,000 per year maintenance and operations budget without undue difficulty.

The committee offered to raise $40,000 in cash or pledges to be paid over a period of five years, which would provide $8,000 a year to support the library. This annual donation meant that for the first five years, the city would only have to add $2,000 from its budget to meet the amount required by a Carnegie grant of $100,000.

On December 17, 1906, the city council passed Ordinance 1331 giving the Little Rock Board of Public Affairs permission to "build, furnish and equip a library, and to receive donations and subscriptions" for it. On February 23, 1907, Mayor Lenon officially requested a grant of $100,000 from Andrew Carnegie. The request was denied, as Carnegie did not think that so much money was needed to build "a suitable Library Building for the city of Little Rock."

Despite this refusal, the Library Committee pressed forward.[27] Mayor Lenon wrote a letter of introduction to Andrew Carnegie for T. H. Bunch, president of the Business Men's League, and Samuel Reyburn. Bunch and Reyburn were going to New York, so they were asked to call on Carnegie to negotiate for the larger grant amount.

Years later, at the request of librarian Vera Snook, Reyburn wrote an essay describing this part of the library's history. Reyburn described a series of meetings in New York that included visits with architect Edward Tilton, who provided rough plans and an estimate of costs of $88,100. According to Reyburn, he tried to persuade Tilton to increase the amount to $100,000, but was unsuccessful.[28] A May 22, 1907, letter from Bunch, who was also chairman of the Public Library Board, gives details of the proposed cost, including construction and furnishings, which comes to the $88,100 figure. Bertram's letter of August 6 confirms Carnegie's willingness to raise the grant amount from $50,000 to that figure.

A handwritten note in the Carnegie correspondence reads simply, "Little Rock, Ark. Increase $38,100 Aug 6/07. RAF advised Feb 20/08." RAF was R. A. Franks of Home Trust Company in Hoboken, New Jersey, who was responsible for disbursing funds for Carnegie's library grants.

Location and Construction Planning

At the November 1906 meeting of the aldermen, resistance was expressed to accepting the Carnegie grant because of the promise it required of the city, seen by some as being "galling obligations." The majority of the discussion focused on choosing the location. Although several locations were discussed, the two most strongly considered were the southwest corner of 8th and Scott streets and a location at 7th and Louisiana streets. J. H. Hollis spoke in favor of the former location because of its "more handsome surroundings," while the latter was less expensive. No decision was made at this meeting.

At successive meetings, the aldermen received the report of the Library Committee in which the committee recommended Lots 10, 11 and 12, Block 67, City of Little Rock, the southwest corner of 7th and Louisiana streets. The committee also had collected donations for the purchase of the site, to add to funds raised earlier by the women's organizations. They turned over to the city a total of $21,746.

The *Arkansas Democrat* referred to the location as a "low, damp, overflowed, undesirably situated piece of property." J. N. Heiskell responded in the *Arkansas Gazette* by writing: "The site does not just now present a very attractive picture since it is covered with various sorts of junk and there is a ditch by it. But within twelve months that same ground will be occupied by a beautiful building, the ground will be terraced and the ditch will be abolished. The building will be set far enough back from the sidewalk to give the proper effect, and the library will be one of the showplaces of the city."[29]

The terms of the subscriptions that funded the purchase of the property and further support of the library required that construction begin before the end of that year. Thus, the city council had to move quickly, and it gave its final approval of the recommendation on December 3, 1907, allowing H. F. Auten to move forward with the purchase. At the same meeting, it approved the contract with Tilton as architect.

Tilton, an award-winning architect known for his designs of public buildings, was good friends with Bertram, who had recommended the architect to many of the towns that were building libraries with Carnegie funds.[30] Tilton pioneered the use of the Open Plan, which located the majority of the popular books on open shelves on the main floor of the library where patrons could browse them instead of having all of the books in closed stacks.

The board gave final approval to the building plans on December 27, and excavation began on December 28.

On February 11, 1908, the council passed Ordinance 1400, to accept the donation of $88,100 from Andrew Carnegie and proceed with the construction process. The ordinance also confirmed the nine-member Board of Trustees and provided that vacancies were to be filled "by election by the city council upon the nomination and recommendation made by the board of trustees hereby constituted."[31]

Although Tilton designed the building, he preferred to contract with local architects to assist with the local arrangements. In Little Rock, he chose Charles Thompson to coordinate the project.

Bids on the construction of the building were reviewed in May, with both Tilton and Thompson present at the meeting. The board accepted contractor W. R. Stewart's bid of $71,390, A. V. Rogoski's bid of $2,415 for plumbing and heating, and the Electric Construction Company's bid of $1,375 for electric wiring.

Although pleased with their success in getting the library initiative before the city council, May Voss thought the women were not getting the credit they deserved for the ultimate success of the effort. In a letter to Carnegie, dated December 8, 1907, she apologizes for not having personally written in some months: "I have wondered if you did not think the ladies who started the movement had grown indifferent, but the aldermen asked that the matter be placed in their hands if the appropriation were made, so we could not take any further steps without their consent and request. I am very glad the businessmen of the city have taken the matter up, but feel that some recognition should be given the efforts of the ladies who work[ed] so hard to bring the matter before the Council in the first place."

African-American Community Excluded

The prospect of having a true public library in Little Rock encouraged members of the African-American community to pursue a similar project. At a May 1909 Board of Trustees meeting, when construction of the library was well under way, John E. Bush—co-founder of the Mosaic Templars of America, an African-American fraternal organization—reported the offer of First Baptist Church, Colored, to donate a lot near Seventh and Gaines streets for the purpose of building "a Negro Library at Little Rock."

Service to the African-American community had been discussed during the initial discussions with the Carnegie Foundation, but information regarding those conversations is sketchy.

In his memoir, Reyburn gave a detailed account of broaching the subject with Bertram, who got angry and said the whole deal was off if the library would not be open to all. According to Reyburn, he and Bertram argued about it, with Bertram telling him that Booker T. Washington would be a guest at Carnegie's home in a coming weekend. Reyburn told Bertram that he would be glad to attend the dinner if he were invited, because after all he often sat down at the table with "old Uncle Joe" and others who had been slaves of his father, but that he wanted to "chose the colored people he sat at dinner with or rubbed shoulders with at the library."

Little Rock's first public library building.

He and Bertram agreed that the question of whether the library should be open to both races in Little Rock would be presented to Washington during his upcoming visit with Carnegie, and that his recommendation would be followed. The two had apparently talked about the possibility that a whites-only library would be built first, and that later "the Carnegie Corporation might see fit to contribute $15,000 or $20,000 to provide a separate library for the colored people." Whether that quasi-promise was part of the question as it was presented to Washington, Reyburn did not say. Washington's recommendation, he said, was that there be separate libraries. "So the Carnegie aid for the library for whites alone," he continued, "we owe to Booker T. Washington."[32] Other research suggests that this question would not have come up in the negotiations unless the local people brought it up, and that Carnegie did not try to use his grants to force integration in Southern cities, as Reyburn had reported.

Reyburn reported that he felt certain a Carnegie grant of $15,000 "could be relied upon." Such a building would be contingent not only on receiving the Carnegie grant, but on the city council appropriating an additional $1,500 "for the support of said Negro Library." The trustees passed resolutions approving the project, pending such approval and support. The "Negro Library" is not mentioned in the trustees' minutes again until 1916, and a separate building for the branch was never built.

Open for Business

Mary Maud Pugsley, who had previous experience at establishing libraries in Wheaton, Illinois, and Traverse City, Michigan, was hired as librarian in May 1909 and began her duties on September 15.[33] Construction on the building was not yet finished, but it had reached the point where Pugsley and Fannie O'Connell, who served as assistant librarian until May 1910, could begin work in the building. With the formal opening already scheduled, they decided to work with a shelf list and a book card for each volume and do formal cataloging as time allowed. The WCA contributed the books from their library, and 100 of the books were added to the shelves in time for the grand opening. The rest of the WCA collection was formally accessioned and catalogued later.

The Little Rock Public Library held an open house for the public on February 1, 1910; on February 2, formal circulation began. At the end of the first day of business, 500 people had applied for library cards. To register, borrowers had to be Little Rock property owners or had to get the signature of a property owner on their application for a card.[34] J. N. Heiskell, a strong supporter of the library and secretary of the Board of Trustees, received library card number 1.

The LRPL librarians used a ledger to register patron names and assign their library card numbers. This page from the first register shows that J. N. Heiskell was the first patron, followed by Mrs. E. G. Wells, Sterling Bond, John Bond, Julia Bennett, and H. M. Bennett.

Heiskell, who had served continuously on the Board of Trustees since before the library opened, received the American Library Association's Trustee Citation in 1957.

---

1 Jeffrey Croteau, "Yet More American Circulating Libraries: A Preliminary Checklist of Brooklyn (New York) Circulating Libraries," *Library History* 22 (November 2006): 171–80.

2 Jane Georgine Woodruff, "William E. Woodruff as Remembered by His Three Daughters." *Arkansas Gazette Centennial Edition*, November 20, 1919.

3 *Arkansas Gazette*, November 8, 1834.

4 *Arkansas Gazette*, June 10, 1870.

5 This corner is the current location of the Arkansas Studies Institute, part of the Main Library campus of the Central Arkansas Library System.

6 This is now the home of the *Arkansas Democrat-Gazette*.

7 *Woman's Cooperative Association Yearbook, 1905–1906*, Small Manuscripts Collection, Butler Center for Arkansas Studies, Arkansas Studies Institute, Little Rock, Arkansas.

8 Adolphine Krause Fletcher was the mother of poet John Gould Fletcher and of Adolphine Fletcher Terry (who served on the Little Rock Public Library Board of Trustees for forty years). Although Mrs. Fletcher strongly supported the library movement, she did not live to see the Little Rock Public Library open, as she died of cancer in 1909. Both Adolphine Fletcher Terry and John Gould Fletcher have branch libraries named after them.

9 *Arkansas Gazette*, February 14, 1897.

10 Sources refer to the association meeting "in their rooms" in City Park, and also, as here, to the "library rooms." They do not make clear whether the meeting rooms and the library rooms were the same location.

11 The fee for juveniles was later raised to 50 cents per year.

12 *Arkansas Gazette,* June 29, 1890.

13 Frances Mitchell Ross, "The New Woman as Club Woman and Social Activist in Turn of the Century Arkansas," *Arkansas Historical Quarterly* 50 (Winter 1991): 317–51.

14 Jennie H. Pillow, then president of the Arkansas Federation of Women's Clubs, *Arkansas Democrat*, January 15, 1898.

15 Carnegie began his library grants in 1881 with a gift to Dunfermline, his hometown in Scotland. His gifts to establish public libraries continued through 1915, when the Carnegie Corporation, which he formed in 1911 to handle his philanthropy, shifted its emphasis to the education of librarians. During these years, Carnegie grants built 2,509 libraries, including 1,679 libraries in 1,412 U.S. communities.

16 George S. Bobinski, *Carnegie Libraries: Their History and Impact on American Public Library Development* (Chicago, IL: American Library Association), 1969.

17 Carnegie, Andrew, *The Autobiography of Andrew Carnegie* (Boston and New York: Houghton Mifflin Co.), 1920.

18 Jesse H. Shera, *Foundations of the Public Library: The Origins of the Public Library Movement in New England 1629–1855*. Hamden, CT: The Shoe String Press, 1974 (originally published by University of Chicago Press, 1947).

19 Much of the information that follows is based on correspondence in the Carnegie Corporation of New York Records, Rare Book and Manuscript Library, Columbia University Libraries, New York, New York, Series II.A.1.a, reel 17. Although correspondence was frequently addressed to Andrew Carnegie directly, responses were always from his secretary, James Bertram. A copy of this file is now available as part of the CALS collection.

20 In the United States, cities and towns are legally creatures of the state; state constitutions and state law define municipalities and their rights and responsibilities.

21 The microfilmed copies of these handwritten letters are almost unreadable. Bertram eventually asked Mrs. Voss to use a typewriter for her correspondence; with their busy schedules, it took too long for them to decipher her handwriting.

22 According to Arkansas law, a "city of the first class" has a population of 2,500 or more, while a second-class city has a population between 500 and 2,500. "Municipal Designations," *The Encyclopedia of Arkansas History & Culture*. http://www.encyclopediaofarkansas.net/encyclopedia/entry-detail.aspx?search=1&entryID=5738 (accessed September 11, 2009).

23 A Carnegie grant required that the city commit to supporting the library with an amount equal to ten percent of the grant received. The $5,000 figure was based on the projected request for a grant of $50,000.

24 *Arkansas Gazette*, January 23, 1906.

25 No mention is made in available sources that this was actually a legal requirement of receiving a Carnegie grant. Research suggests that cities often misunderstood the details of the process, frequently assuming that Carnegie had legal recourse once the grant was given to enforce the requirement when, in fact, he did not. In some situations, he may have suspended new grants to a state where cities failed to keep their commitment; however, by the time the discussion came up in regard to Little Rock, the Carnegie Corporation was no longer giving new grants for library buildings.

26 Samuel W. Reyburn, "Early History of the Little Rock Public Library," ca. 1938, available in the CALS collection.

27 The council had appointed a Library Committee that included Reyburn, T. H. Bunch, H. F. Auten, and Chris Ledwidge. Ordinance 1360, passed on April 29, 1907, established this group as the Little Rock Public Library Board of Trustees, giving them permission and authority to pursue funding with Carnegie and continue with establishing the library.

28 Although this essay has served as a primary source of information for institutional history, further research suggests that the passage of time may have blurred Reyburn's memory of the events. Reyburn essentially put himself in the center of the process. His tone implied this sentiment (common for a man of his generation): The women have done a great job up until now, but it's time for the men to take over and get the job done. Reyburn, "Early History of the Little Rock Public Library."

29 *Arkansas Democrat*, December 4, 1907; *Arkansas Gazette*, December 11, 1907.

30 Tilton designed more than 100 libraries in the United States and Canada, many of which were funded by the Carnegie Foundation. James Bertram wrote letters of introduction for Tilton to many of the local library committees, which gave Tilton a distinct advantage in securing commissions. Lisa B. Mausolf and Elizabeth Durfee Hengen, "Edward Lippincott Tilton: A Monograph on His Architectural Practice." Currier Museum of Art, 2007, http://www.nh.gov/nhdhr/publications/documents/etilton_monograph.pdf.

31 *Digest of the City of Little Rock, Arkansas: Embracing the Ordinances and Resolutions of a General Character Passed by the City Council of Said City up to and Including the Session of September 21, 1914 / Comp. and Digested by Authority of the City Council by Harry C. Hale of the Little Rock Bar* (Little Rock: Democrat Printing & Lithographing Co., 1915).

32 Reyburn's version of the events has been repeated several times throughout the years as a part of the library's history, based only on his essay. Reyburn, the son and grandson of slave owners, wrote his description at a time when the question of equal access was already being discussed; he may have given a personal and defensive shape to the details as he recalled them. Board of Trustees' minutes from 1909, two years after the meetings with Bertram, suggest that the two had at least discussed the possibility of funding a branch for the black community.

33 *Public Libraries, A Monthly Review of Library Matters and Methods* (Chicago, IL: Library Bureau, 1904, 1905 and 1912 annual reports).

34 According to the 1910 census, Little Rock had a population of 45,951, so approximately 1% of the town's population applied for a library card on the first day of business and 2.5% had applied by the end of the first year. By 1915, the number of applications was up to 9,700.

chapter three

GROWING PAINS: 1911–1925

"The daily desk work, reference work, the effort to increase the reading of better books, the sympathy with each individual that goes into the building up of a reading public, these cannot be tabulated nor do the results show in figures. That a higher standard of citizenship and that a better civic life may grow up among us is our aim and our justification."

MARY MAUD PUGSLEY, LIBRARIAN, LITTLE ROCK PUBLIC LIBRARY, 1912

Now that the proponents had succeeded in erecting the Little Rock Public Library (LRPL), they had to turn their attention to running the operation. The collection at the time the library opened amounted to approximately 2,500 books, with only a portion of them catalogued. The staff consisted of one librarian, one assistant librarian, and a janitor.

Part of the process of cataloging books involved accessioning the materials, which meant that the librarians had to give each item a tracking number and record bibliographic information including title, author, number of pages, and other data that would allow them to identify each unique item. Librarians used special archival registers to record this information, and these registers provided the basis for the card catalog that was available to the public.

The librarian also kept track of circulation information by filling out a monthly report showing how many books were checked out by both adults and children.

Children's programming began during the first year the library was open. Dorothy D. Lyon, previously children's librarian at the Cleveland Public Library, joined the LRPL staff as children's librarian in September 1910. For the next few months, story time sessions were held on the Saturday nearest Halloween, Thanksgiving, and Christmas. This program proved so popular that beginning in

January 1911, story time met every Saturday morning. By 1913, the space in the corner of the children's section of the library was no longer adequate, and a special room was constructed on the top floor of the library

During its first winter, the library responded creatively when "a street gang threatened the peace and windows of the library." They formed a boys' club that met once a week for activities and refreshments; Pugsley said this action "solved the problem and the boys were now our defenders."[1]

The cost of constructing the library totaled less than the Carnegie grant, and the library was left with $186.33. Reyburn, who served as treasurer of the grant funds, asked Bertram if the funds could be used to purchase a stereopticon and collection of slides. Bertram agreed to the use of the funds, which provided an opportunity for the library to offer adult programming. According to the 1916 annual report, the stereopticon and the collection of slides made possible a series of free lectures, the first of many talks with speakers drawn from a variety of fields of interest.

Statewide Efforts for Libraries

During its first year of operation, the Little Rock Public Library took a leadership role in library development in the entire state. Certainly, this leadership came in part from a sense of responsibility as the library in the largest city, which was also the state capital. But it also came from the understanding that some needs of the LRPL could only be met through actions of the legislature, which would require statewide support.

In 1909, the American Library Association (ALA) published recommendations for a model library law. They included three key points: "careful and consecutive management," "a sure and steady revenue," and "a central agency for supervision and promotion." Another important point was that funds generated through whatever tax method was established should be under the control of the library board, and not the municipal or local governing group.[2]

In December 1910, Pugsley proposed a meeting of librarians from around the state with the goal of persuading the state legislature to approve state funding for public libraries. With this initial step, the Little Rock Public Library staff and trustees joined with the staff and trustees of the Fort Smith Public Library in an appeal to librarians and library supporters to form a state library association. The first meeting of the nascent organization was held on January 26, 1911, at the Little Rock Public Library. The ALA sent Dr. Arthur E. Bostwick, librarian of the St. Louis Public Library, to guide the process.[3]

At this organizational meeting, the new association prepared an appeal to the Arkansas State Legislature to pass new library legislation. The bill that was presented would increase the amount that could be appropriated by cities from ¼ mill to ½ mill, still within the overall limit of 5 mills for a city budget. The law was approved by the legislature on April 7, 1911.

Although this was a step forward, it still did not allow a dedicated tax for libraries. The amount that cities would allocate to their public library was still discretionary, and many people did not see the library as a legal responsibility of the city in the same way as roads and utilities.

Transitions and Growth

With the library in a strong position, Mary Pugsley resigned effective December 15, 1912, to take a position as reference librarian at the public library in Newark, New Jersey. Dorothy Lyon replaced Pugsley, and she served in that position until March 31, 1918.

Despite the comparatively low salaries the LRPL was able to pay, the library was fortunate to have head librarians with training in library science during its developmental years. Some other staff members either had training in library science or took advantage of summer school opportunities for library training. This proved a great benefit, not just to the Little Rock library, but to library work throughout the state. The Little Rock staff passed on their skills by providing training opportunities for librarians from other Arkansas cities and towns. For example, in 1914, librarians from Morrilton and Arkadelphia worked and studied at the LRPL.[4] By sharing their experience and training, the Little Rock staff helped libraries around the state grow both in quality and in quantity.

The growth of library service around the state helped the LRPL in another way, by relieving it from the extra expense of providing service beyond the borders of the city. The 1,847 new borrowers added in 1914 included people from as far away as Forrest City (St. Francis County), El Dorado (Union County), Altus (Franklin County), and Pine Bluff (Jefferson County). Non-resident cards required the signature of a property owner from Little Rock, and the borrower paid the postage to have the books mailed.[5] Such service whetted the appetite of people from around the state for the service of traveling libraries.

The librarians also took portions of the book collection out to public schools during the school year, rotating them every three months. For example, the librarians listed Centennial, Garland, Robert E. Lee, Rightsell, Mitchell, Woodruff, and Forest Park schools as "school branches" in 1914.

The library's book collection continued to grow, largely through the generosity of private citizens. The family of U. M. Rose, the founder of Rose Law Firm, donated his private collection of more than 7,000 volumes to the library in 1913. The trustees hired Laura Brower, whose experience at the Washington DC Public Library gave her the skills needed to process this very scholarly collection. The collection was catalogued and officially presented to the library in a ceremony on November 21, 1914. The collection, which included 2,000 books in French and German, occupied an entire room in the northwest corner of the library building. Louisa Watkins Wright Loughborough's[6] collection of an additional 300 books in French was added to the books in the Rose Room in 1919.

The U. M. Rose book collection represents the largest single donation of materials the library has received.   Photo by Michael Keckhaver

The books left from the Mercantile/Marquand/YMCA library were taken out of storage in 1913 and given to the public library. The librarians examined them and said that they would be able to use some immediately, some could be used after repair, and others were in too poor of a condition and would be discarded. The last of these books were accessioned into the library's collection in 1916.[7]

Financial Struggles

During the first decade of the library's existence, its financial support from the city's budget fell short, not only by the amount needed, but also by the amount the city council had committed to when it accepted the Carnegie grant.

The Carnegie Corporation, using the annual reports, followed up on whether or not cities that had received grants kept their commitments to appropriate ten percent of the grant amount for library operations and maintenance. In early 1916, with four full years of records available, Bertram pursued the matter in a letter to Samuel Reyburn. Bertram's calculations showed that in four years, the city had provided only $23,524, when it should have provided $35,240 ($8,810 per year).

The library planners in Little Rock had assumed that the Carnegie Corporation had a legal penalty for cities that did not meet their financial commitment. But no such penalty existed. Carnegie and Bertram operated instead on the basis that city leaders could be pressured and shamed into keeping their financial commitments. Bertram's challenge to Reyburn in 1916 centered mainly on the fact that the city's pledged word was not being honored, and also on the fact that it was mostly Reyburn's persuasion that had led to the greater grant amount. He pointed out that the amount actually given by the city for running the library would have been adequate if the city had accepted the $50,000 grant and not asked for the larger amount.

Between the correspondence with Reyburn and an interview in New York with Charles Taylor, then the mayor of Little Rock, Bertram accepted the city's commitment to meet the pledge for 1916, as well as make up the amount it was short in the first few years. Librarian Dorothy Lyon reported to Bertram in June 1917 that during the previous year, not only had the library received its full appropriation, but had been allowed $1,000 above that amount, and this during a year in which decreased revenues had forced cuts in every other city department.

Establishing the Colored Branch

The question of the need for library service in the black community came up again, prompted by actions from within the community. Carrie Still Shepperson, an African-American teacher at the Capitol Hill School and an advocate for improved education, set out to do something about the lack of an adequate library at her school. From 1916 to 1918, she staged student presentations of Shakespeare to raise funds to buy library books for the school. These presentations may well have been a factor in bringing the need for library service in the black community into the public eye.[8]

In July 1916, when Little Rock mayor Charles Taylor talked with Bertram at the Carnegie Corporation offices in New York, he raised the question about the possibility of an additional grant to finance construction of a branch library for the black community. He had made public appeals for contributions within the white community but without much success.

By this time, the Carnegie Corporation was moving away from making grants for library buildings, focusing instead on training for librarians. The only building grants being made were ones that had already been promised. Bertram told Taylor that there had been no promise on the part of the Carnegie Corporation to fund a branch for the black community in Little Rock.[9]

A year after Mayor Taylor's visit with Bertram, Dorothy Lyon asked him to approach Bertram again, after members of the black community had raised funds to purchase a site in the hopes of having a branch library. Even though appeals within the white community had fallen short, public appeals endorsed by the ministerial alliance and the Negro Citizens League had yielded support, although not enough for a building. Nevertheless, the need was recognized, and the project moved forward.[10]

On April 2, 1917, city ordinance 2400 authorized the employment of a library assistant to work at a branch library. The Colored Branch of the library opened in June 1917 in rented space in a building on 9th Street that was owned by Scipio Jones, a prominent African-American attorney. The branch was equipped with a desk, tables and chairs, and shelving that could accommodate 2,000 books. The initial collection consisted of approximately 1,200 books—an equal mix of duplicates culled from the main library and books purchased specifically for the branch.

A three-member "Negro board" was elected in 1917 to advise the LRPL's Board of Trustees. The initial members of this board were Bishop J. M. Connor, Rev. J. P. Robinson, and Dr. J. G. Thornton. Five years later, the number was increased to five with the addition of Rev. J. M. B. Michelle and Dr. R. J. Meaddough. This board served solely as an advisory group. The board was never officially eliminated; it simply ceased functioning as various members left it and were not replaced.[11]

The first librarian of the Colored Branch was Caroline Rebecca Stephens, daughter of Charlotte Stephens, the first African-American teacher in Little Rock. The library included both a children's department and an adult division.

The Colored Branch was the only public library service available to the black community in Little Rock for almost thirty-five years, and it remained an integral part of the community for another twenty years after the main library desegregated.

The Calm before the Storm

After the establishment of the Colored Branch, the library settled into a period of stable existence. The library staff continued to struggle to expand the collection and library services with its limited budget, but this period remained largely uneventful. Beatrice Prall from Hope (Hempstead County) replaced Dorothy Lyon as librarian, and Etta C. Washington replaced Caroline Stephens at the Colored Branch.

Washington revamped the hours at the Colored Branch, which had been open from 2:00 to 6:00 p.m. and from 7:00 to 9:00 p.m., to offer continuous service from 2:00 to 8:00 p.m., which was more convenient for the patrons—especially the college students who depended on the library for collateral reading for their classes.[12]

In 1923, the library received a $2,500 bequest—which was a sizeable gift at that time—from Sarah H. Henley of Chicago. Henley had come to Little Rock as a teacher during Reconstruction years and had taught in black schools. She left a share of her estate to the city, to be used for library service that would be open to all the people of the city.

The American Library Association held its 1923 national conference in Hot Springs (Garland County). At that meeting, Mrs. D. L. Phillips, a member of the Edelweiss Club of Little Rock, spoke on the service provided to the local women's clubs by the Little Rock Public Library. She lauded her "own Little Rock library, its capable administration and its wonderful service to the community."[13]

She said that the library, once "a bookkeeping institution, jealously guarding its treasures, has evolved into a dispensary of a relief fund for starving minds." Phillips was especially appreciative of the work of the librarians, who "give unstintedly [sic], their time and assistance, often weary, always courteous." This was especially important in a place like Arkansas, distant and isolated as it was from "the large centers of culture." She spoke of the debt that club women owed to "the patient, harassed librarians, true missionaries in the cause of advancement of knowledge."[14]

In the 1924 annual report, Beatrice Prall highlighted the extent to which the LRPL provided services to all of Pulaski County and the large number of requests it received. She suggested several ways that such service could be provided and indicated the staff's willingness to do as much as they could along these lines: "This is the day of the county unit idea, and the library is feeling this impetus to a kindred association and interest."

By the time another year had passed, Prall had left her position with the library to become the librarian for the Arkansas Free Library Service Bureau,[15] opening the door for a library crusader who would steer the library through the next twenty years of growth and development—Vera Snook.

---

1 Pugsley's 1912 annual report, prepared in December 1912. After-school activities in today's branch libraries deal with a similar situation, the need to keep visiting students busy after the end of the school day.

2 William F. Yust, *Library Legislation*, reprint of *Manual of Library Economy (1911), Chapter IX* (Chicago, IL: American Library Association Publishing Board, 1921).

3 Bostwick was already familiar with the work in Little Rock, as the Board of Trustees engaged him in 1908 to review and approve the architect's plans for the inside of the building. Arthur E. Bostwick, *The American Public Library* (New York: D. Appleton and Company, 1910).

4 1914 Little Rock Public Library annual report.

5 By 1916, the requirement had changed from requiring a property owner to sign an application to requiring the signature of "an adult permanent resident of the city." 1916 LRPL annual report.

6 Louisa Loughborough, a pioneer in the field of historic preservation in Arkansas, founded the Arkansas Territorial Restoration (now the Historic Arkansas Museum).

7 According to the 1916 annual report, 148 books from the Marquand collection were accessioned during that year. An article in the *Arkansas Gazette*, July 22, 1971, stated that a bank account with the First National Bank in the name of the Marquand Library was still on the bank's books and had activity as late as 1944. As part of an audit that closed such old and inactive accounts, the $283 remaining in the account was given to the library, which, Director Alice Gray said, would buy books with the funds.

8 "Carrie Lena Fambro Still Shepperson (1872–1927)," *The Encyclopedia of Arkansas History & Culture*. http://www.encyclopediaofarkansas.net/encyclopedia/entry-detail.aspx?search=1&entryID=1763 (accessed September 11, 2009).

9 Rosebud Harris Tillman, "The History of Public Library Service to Negroes in Little Rock, Arkansas, 1917–1951" (MLS thesis, School of Library Service, Atlanta, GA, 1953).

10 Tillman, "The History of Public Library Service to Negroes."

11 Tillman, "The History of Public Library Service to Negroes."

12 Two historically black colleges, Philander Smith College and Arkansas Baptist College, were in the neighborhood of the branch library, as was Dunbar Junior College, part of the program of Dunbar High School.

13 *Arkansas Gazette*, April 28, 1923.

14 *Arkansas Gazette*, April 28, 1923.

15 The Arkansas Free Library Service Bureau was a state program established by the legislature in 1921.

chapter four

THE VERA SNOOK YEARS,
1926–1948

"The public library serves all purposes of civic life—industrial, social, religious, and recreational. It assists with the education of the young and continues that of the adult. It is truly American, presenting to the native American and the foreign-born alike the ideals of government. It is the world's largest educational system."[1]

FRANKLIN D. ROOSEVELT, 1937

The success and growth of any non-profit, public service organization depends heavily on key people who step forward when they are needed and who continue to serve in spite of difficulties and frustrations. For more than two decades, during a time of political, social, and economic struggles, Vera Snook was that key person for the Little Rock Public Library and for the public library movement in the state. Snook was a strong force not only in the city library, but also in the establishment of the Pulaski County Library and in the push to establish the Arkansas Library Commission.

Snook became librarian of the LRPL in January 1926. Snook had served as librarian at the Reddick Library in her hometown of Ottawa, Illinois, from 1914 to 1922. As early as 1919, she felt she had accomplished all that she could in Ottawa and was looking for a position that would be more of a challenge. In 1922, she took a position at the Lincoln County Library in Libby, Montana, where she served until she came to Little Rock.

At the library in Ottawa, Snook said that she had "a progressive board, a well trained public, prospects of a larger appropriation and very satisfactory coopera-tion with the schools, clubs, and various organizations."[2] In addition, circulation had more than doubled under her leadership.

Vera Snook

Snook no doubt had similar goals for the Little Rock library. She quickly learned, however, that navigating the political dynamics in Little Rock was a very different situation. Nevertheless, Snook remained outspoken and determined in presenting the needs of the library to the decision makers. In a September 1928 letter to James Bertram of the Carnegie Corporation, she explained her approach: "Arkansas is not a rich state but large sums of money are spent on some things which offer insignificant returns....I have always found that as long as a librarian accepts a humble place no city council will offer her the necessary funds for better library service."

The Struggle Begins

Snook's letter to the mayor and the city council regarding the proposed 1927 budget, the first one she prepared, must have alerted them to the fact that they were facing a new era. As with the women who pushed for the founding of a public library in Little Rock, Snook would not rest until she had secured the funding needed to provide quality library service for the people of the city. She wrote in a letter to the city council accompanying a statistical report: "The question of our budget for the coming year is not so much a matter of how much I think we should have, or how much any one [sic] thinks we can have, but rather how much can be allowed from the city's funds for library work. The members of the council know that our appropriation is very small compared with other libraries and that there is a direct ratio between appropriation and achievement."

She followed with a comparison of Little Rock's library with libraries in other U.S. cities with a similar population, showing how meager Little Rock was in funding and also in circulation and collection.[3] She then considered the various portions of the budget and what could or could not be done to modify expenditures.

When she discussed the amount budgeted for staff, she detailed what the staff was currently accomplishing and pointed out that without additional staff, they could not provide the services that the public and the schools were asking for. Thus began the struggle between Snook and the city over adequate funding for the library—a struggle that continued until passage of a dedicated library tax took the matter out of the hands of city government.

By 1930, the appropriation for the library had inched its way up to $26,102, with $6,245 spent on acquiring books.

Politics and Governance

Snook turned frequently for assistance and consolation to the leaders of the library school at the University of Illinois, where she had received her training. In this correspondence, she frequently lamented her constant struggle with the local politicians.

She reported in 1931 that she had, without intending to, angered every mayor since she had been in Little Rock: "If I attempt to maintain a library that wins the approval of my reading public I invariably call down upon my head

From Carnegie to Cyberspace: 100 Years at the Central Arkansas Library System

the indignation of some of the members of our city council. If I could conduct a library without any expenditures I might not have any trouble."

A few months later, she reported, "I should not be in a library where I have to take orders from city politicians. I am having a round with the new mayor. I hope someday that this library will be administered entirely by a board chosen from the citizenship at large according to fitness and that an alderman who boasts that he is chairman of the library committee of the council because he has never read a book will not be in a position to recommend or dictate library policies."

Phineas Windsor, her mentor from the school, advised her, "When you have a Mayor who will rather deliberately try to starve a public library…you will either have to get rid of him or else you will have to become influential enough to make him fear you politically. That's often a hard thing for a librarian to do."

Snook found herself in a position doomed to be caught up in controversy. Act 177 of 1931 provided for a five-member library committee appointed by the mayor, so the city council had a library committee and the library had a board of trustees. These two factions had conflicting opinions on which group more appropriately made policy and financial decisions for the library. As long as the library's budget came from a portion of the whole city budget, the mayor and the council had a measure of control over library operations. Even after the law allowed, and the people had approved, a dedicated property tax millage for library funding, the mayor attempted to establish more direct control over the appointment of trustees.

Struggles, Acquisitions, and the Arkansas Room

While Snook struggled with the politics of library governance, Etta Washington struggled to make the Colored Branch more accessible to the African-American community. The librarian's 1929 annual report stated that the Colored Branch had moved to a rented room over the Children's Drug Store on 9th Street.

Washington reported a decline in circulation, which she felt was in part because the library was on the second floor. She asked for a new location that would be on the first floor and thus more accessible. Indeed, annual reports showed that she frequently requested a more accessible location. Another factor contributing to the drop in circulation, Washington felt, was that the branch did not have any new books, and what they did have was in poor condition.[4] Snook acknowledged that few books had been added to the collection in several years.

Washington's concerns came on the cusp of the Great Depression, a time that challenged all institutions and citizens in the country. Despite the city's overall financial struggles, Snook continued to lobby for additional funding, fueling the continued conflict between the librarian and the city.

Although conflict continued between Snook and the city government, public support of the library continued to grow, both through donations of materials and through political support.

In the earliest years of the library, books about Arkansas and books by Arkansas authors were shelved separately in what the 1915 annual report referred to as the "Arkansas Corner." According to this report, the library was attempting to add "pamphlets, folders, programs, yearbooks and pictures" that would help in preserving Arkansas history.

The Arkansas Corner expanded to become the Arkansas Room when former Governor Charles Brough bequeathed his collection of approximately 3,000 volumes of Arkansiana to the library in 1934.[5]

The federal Office of Education, in cooperation with the American Library Association, published a collection of 660 pamphlets on public policy issues, which they distributed through libraries in thirty cities, including the LRPL.

The Citizens Library Association (CLA) formed in 1936 with Rabbi Ira Sanders as chairman. The CLA was composed of library patrons and supporters drawn from "leading civic, educational, professional, and business groups."[6] Its purpose was to promote interest in the library and to interpret its work to the community. Its projects included raising funds to buy books and a bookmobile, as well as campaigning for an increased appropriation for the library from the city council. The group also worked to get a state constitutional amendment passed allowing a dedicated library tax.

Expansion

The financial problems of the LRPL were compounded by the financial setbacks experienced by the entire nation during the Great Depression. As support from the city dwindled, the library operated on a smaller and smaller budget. Ironically, this decline in library support came at a time when more and more people were turning to the library for vocational help as well as for recreation.

In January 1937, a bond issue, initiated by the CLA, came before the voters to fund a $45,000 addition to the LRPL. Plans for the addition included an auditorium, additional stacks, and offices. The Little Rock Federation of Women's Clubs voted to give its support to the proposal. The library, they pointed out, had recently been forced to decline the gift of a private collection due to lack of space.

The city officials wanted the Works Progress Administration (WPA) to accept the project, so that the cost could be shared—the city would pay $25,000 and the federal government the other $20,000. Snook was relentless in her push to get a set appropriation for the library and what might be considered more adequate funding. In March 1938, she spoke of the "six famine years" that both the city and the library had endured. Her two principal concerns were improving circulation and increasing the book collection.

In December 1937, the city council authorized issuing $25,000 in bonds and noted that the WPA had accepted the project and approved a total cost of $56,000 for the addition.

Construction on the annex began on January 5, 1938. The addition, which consisted of three floors and a basement, more than doubled the floor space of the library, increasing it from 23,000 to 53,000 square feet. Planners estimated that it would house approximately 30,000 additional books.

In April 1939, the annex was completed. The library held a week-long celebration to mark the opening of the annex, beginning with a dedication on the evening of April 26. The next day, the library held an authors' tea honoring Arkansas writers. Other events included special exhibits of art and books.

Early Friends of the Library

The city participated in several WPA projects, including the Lamar Porter Athletic Field (1934) and the Museum of Fine Arts (1936), which created an additional drain on available funds. By 1938, the city's funds were so depleted that it made no appropriation for library books that year.

During this time, the Citizens Library Association worked to provide additional financial support to the library. Foster Vineyard, assistant general agent for the Aetna Life Insurance Company, was elected chairman of the CLA on March 11, 1938, succeeding Rabbi Ira Sanders. The CLA committed to raise $500 toward the purchase of a bookmobile for the Pulaski County Library. That same year, the organization changed its name to the Greater Little Rock Citizens' Library Association, with hopes of gathering support from citizens of North Little Rock and the rest of Pulaski County.

The group decided to conduct a membership drive to help raise money for the library. They set membership dues at $1 for regular members and $5 for patron-level members. Vineyard said, "This organization is sponsoring interest in the Little Rock Public Library, but it recognizes the fact that the library is an institution supported by the city and is not dependent upon public subscriptions for its maintenance."[7]

The group mailed out more than 1,000 letters inviting people to join the organization. They placed a large poster in the rotunda of the library and added the names of members as they joined. The organization also formed a memorial book collection committee, legislative committee, bookmobile committee, and fractions committee to help provide support to the library.

Living on a Shoestring Budget

The librarians compensated for their lack of financial resources with creative methods for developing the collection and providing programming. The newly expanded space gave them room to expand some of their programming. For example, the Summer Reading Program, one of the more popular youth activities, encouraged children to

Rosalind and Ruth Kramer add arrows to Robin Hood's target to represent the books they read during the summer reading program.
Photo courtesy of the *Arkansas Democrat-Gazette*

continue to develop their reading skills outside of the regular school year. In 1938, the library chose a Robin Hood theme. Ida Mae Hagin, the children's librarian, said they chose the theme because Robin Hood had come into special

The Boy Scouts of America organization was founded on February 8, 1910, just six days after the grand opening of the Little Rock Public Library. In 1939, the library partnered with the local scout organization to create the Boy Scout Nook. This photo shows John Hegner, Carl Dillaha, and Charles Marak using the nook to expand their scouting knowledge.

Photo courtesy of the
Arkansas Democrat-Gazette

prominence through the new Warner Bros. motion picture *The Adventures of Robin Hood*, which starred Errol Flynn. Participants placed an arrow on a target for each book read, achieving a "bulls-eye" for reading ten books.

Snook tried to overcome the lack of funding for collection development by reaching out to special-interest groups to add materials to the library. For example, she created the Boy Scout Nook in the children's department in 1939. The nook contained copies of the Scout handbook, merit badge pamphlets, *Boys' Life* magazine, *Scouting* magazine, and other materials furnished by the Scout council.

Snook also worked with the Musical Coterie to create an audio collection for the library. In 1940, the Musical Coterie, in cooperation with Mrs. Frank Vaughn, presented a concert series at Robinson Auditorium and donated a percentage of the proceeds to purchase a phonograph for the library and an initial collection of eleven classical music albums. The new auditorium in the annex served double duty as the listening room because it was far enough away from the rest of the building that records could be played without disturbing readers.

One cooperative program Snook used to increase resources involved the State Board of Education, which provided $1,200 for the purchase of new books to be kept in the schools during the school year and at the library during the summer months.[8]

However, the Colored Branch continued to have space woes. By 1937, the branch was housed at 922 West 9th at the edge of the 9th Street business district and away from the residential areas. This location, on the second floor of the Raines Building, was accessible only by a narrow set of stairs. Circulation continued to suffer because of the inconvenience.

Little Rock Library for Negroes

The Negro branch occupies this building on West Sixteenth Street.

The exterior of the Colored
Branch on 16th Street.
Clipping courtesy of the
Arkansas Democrat-Gazette

In 1941, the branch relocated to 1413 High Street, at the corner of 16th and High Street (now Dr. Martin Luther King Blvd.). The new location consisted of two rooms in the W. G. Hall Building, a retail center built in 1917. The building had two storefront locations facing High Street, each about 1,900 square feet, and four spaces, each about 840 square feet, facing 16th Street. Each retail space had a direct door to the sidewalk and a service entrance at the back. The library branch occupied the last two spaces on the side facing 16th Street. At first, the branch library used only the one room at 1413 W. 16th; in 1945, it expanded to include the room at 1415, giving it a room for the children's collection and a separate room for the adult department.

This location proved much more convenient for patrons of the branch library; it was closer to the residential areas, within walking distance for many patrons, and near both Arkansas Baptist College and Philander Smith College.

Amendment 33 Brings Dedicated Funding

In November 1940, voters approved Amendment 33, an initiative petition that permitted cities with populations of more than 5,000 to vote for a property tax, not to exceed one mill, dedicated to library service. With the passage of the new amendment, community supporters in Little Rock came together with the Greater Little Rock Library Association to support a tax millage for the library. William Sprott, curator of the Little Rock Zoo, broadcast from the cage of Ruth the elephant in support of the millage.

The Greater Little Rock Library Association also helped provide programming resources. On May 2, 1941, the association sponsored a lecture by widely known journalist and broadcaster William L. Shirer, five months after he had been forced to leave Germany.[9] This appearance occurred during the campaign for approval of the library millage and served to present the value of library services to the people of the city.

William Sprott and Ruth the elephant.
Photo courtesy of the *Arkansas Democrat-Gazette*

The millage law passed in 1941, and, at long last, the Little Rock Public Library had a fixed revenue stream that was not subject to decisions of the city council. After the millage law was passed, bookkeeping and budgeting work for the library was no longer done at City Hall. The library hired Margaret Burkhead to serve as executive secretary. She accepted the tax funds collected by the city and handled all of the library's finances.

During the next decade, Burkhead gradually came to oversee all of the business-related tasks for the organization, although her work was not limited to that. Her duties, she explained in a 1952 newspaper interview, could include "ejecting a drunk from the building; climbing out on the roof to inspect work being done; and wielding the mop when a downstairs room flooded, and the janitor was not to be found."[10]

Almost as soon as the library secured the dedicated millage, conflict developed over how the library's Board of Trustees was structured and how vacancies were filled. Mayor Charles Moyer contended that Act 177 of 1931, which provided for a five-member board appointed by the mayor, superseded the law under which the library was formed and had been functioning.

After the city council passed an ordinance that would test the question in the courts, trustee Charles T. Coleman wrote a paper in which he expressed concern that the mayor was trying to take control of the library budget through appointment of members to the Board of Trustees. The estimated tax stream from the library tax was $40,000 per year, which would be handled entirely by the library staff and the Board of Trustees. Coleman contended that Moyer raised the issue of changing the governance only to get control of that money.

Rather than let the matter reach the courts, the two groups agreed to compromise. The agreement provided that the library would have a five-member board, appointed by the mayor on the recommendation of the board; it also gave the Board of Trustees complete control over the library and its tax revenue.

Just when Vera Snook should have been able to enjoy the fruits of her labors, the Japanese attack on Pearl Harbor threw the country into another period of turmoil. As the country mobilized for war, the library extended its hours to include Sunday afternoons to accommodate soldiers at Camp Joseph T. Robinson (formerly Camp Pike), which was serving as a replacement training center, and for the wartime workers who could not get there during regular business hours.[11] The soldiers especially appreciated the music room and were surprised at the size of the library's record collection.[12]

Adeline Lee, Pvt. Ray Kaltenbrann from St. Louis, and Sgt. Jim Hamilton from Dodge City listen to records in the music room.

Photo courtesy of the *Arkansas Democrat-Gazette*

From Carnegie to Cyberspace: 100 Years at the Central Arkansas Library System

Postwar Years

Vera Snook remained vigilant in her efforts, pointing out that, although the millage provided dedicated funds for the library, more funding was needed to create a first-class library. She renewed her efforts as the war years came to a close. In her December 12, 1946, newspaper column, she said that the American Library Association recommended funding of $1 per capita to provide limited library service, $1.50 per capita for reasonably good service, and $2 per capita for high-quality service. She estimated that the one-mill tax would produce approximately fifty cents per capita.

Despite Snook's gloomy pronouncements regarding funding, the LRPL was a source of pride for the public. Snook had often spoken of the strength of the library staff and the high proportion of them who had specific library training. For those who were skilled and enjoyed the work but lacked such training, Snook helped them find ways to fill this void through summer training programs.[13]

The public seemed to enjoy the ambiance of the building as much as they liked the competent staff. A 1947 column in the *Arkansas Gazette* described the LRPL, featuring the "Lena Latkin reading room where upholstered furniture simply invites a person to make himself comfortable and enjoy a book. The paneled room with its soft lights looks more like a library in a fine home than the reading rooms that are typical of public libraries. And there are ash trays. Pictures throughout the building—even in the stack rooms—make the whole place appear livable."[14]

The Colored Branch could not be described in such glowing terms. Some people questioned whether the Colored Branch was serving a need because it had low circulation figures. In fact, until the late 1940s, when the rise in black activism forced a more honest look at the token service provided to African Americans in a number of areas, the leadership of the library treated the branch as little more than a deposit station for books.

In her 1930 report to the mayor, Snook included circulation statistics for the Colored Branch, but also stated that "Little Rock has no branch libraries." Another time she referred to the librarian at the branch as essentially "a custodian of books." These comments demonstrate that Snook did not give the Colored Branch the encouragement and leadership needed to help it serve its patrons well.

Etta Washington served as librarian at the Colored Branch until 1946, when failing health forced her to resign. Fannie Dukes Bryant, a graduate of Dunbar Junior College and of Spelman College in Atlanta, Georgia, briefly served as librarian following Washington's resignation. In 1947, Louise Washington Smith, daughter of Etta Washington, became the new librarian. Smith, who had worked with her mother for many years, studied at Philander Smith College and also received library training at Spelman College under a Rosenwald Foundation Grant in 1930.[15] A Dunbar Junior College student assisted Smith for two hours a day. Later, local high school students worked as pages in the Colored Branch.[16]

According to library policy, books requested by patrons at the Colored Branch would be provided for them from the main library. In her 1941 study of library service to blacks in the South, Eliza Atkins Gleason noted that this

LENA LATKIN MEMORIAL ROOM

The plaque on the fireplace in the Lena Latkin Memorial Room read: "This room is dedicated by the citizens and the school children of Pulaski County, to the memory of Lena Latkin, 1886–1933, teacher, dreamer, worker who moulded [sic] the youth of Pulaski County for 25 years in ways which we who revered her would steadfastly follow." Those words, carved into the heavy walnut woodwork between the fireplace and the mantle of the LRPL reading room, honor Lena Latkin, who served as assistant superintendent of the Pulaski County elementary schools from 1924 to 1933. She was known for helping students secure loans for higher education and also as a supporter of the Little Rock Public Library. She helped establish the county book-mobile program. The Lena Latkin Memorial Room was established in her memory after her death.

Photo courtesy of the *Arkansas Democrat-Gazette*

An article in the June 13, 1948, issue of the *Arkansas Gazette* noted some of the books available at the Colored Branch, including:

- Bond: *Negro Education in Alabama*
- Cheney: *Men Who Have Walked with God*
- Dunlap and Williamson: *Institutions of Higher Learning among Negroes in the United States*
- Myers: *History of Bigotry in the United States*
- Odum: *Race and Humours of Race*
- Ojike: *My Africa*
- Wilson: *Liberia*

The majority of the books added to the collection at the Colored Branch were written by or about African Americans. "Mainstream" books had to be requested from the main library.

arrangement, where it existed, was often defined as being available "under special request," and the determination was made by the main library and treated as a privilege and not the regular service.[17]

The Little Rock Public Library generally used the list of books requested by patrons as a guide when it selected and purchased books. The fact that few specific requests for books were received from patrons at the branch library was interpreted to mean that the members of the community had little interest in reading or in using the library. Even the employees at the branch had no way of knowing what books were available at the main library, which of course limited patrons' ability to borrow the books. In addition, the policy did not provide access to reference books, which did not leave the library.

A survey undertaken in 1946 by the Little Rock Urban League evaluated the library service at the branch and found several deficiencies, traceable to lack of support from the main library and from the city. "The Little Rock Library Board appears to have a further responsibility to Negro citizens…in the area of equal accommodations and services."[18]

The End of an Era

Vera Snook died of a heart attack on March 1, 1948, at the age of sixty, after twenty-two years of service to the Little Rock Public Library.

Rabbi Ira Sanders, then president of the Library Board of Trustees, issued a statement saying, "In the passing of Vera Snook Little Rock's intellectual and cultural life has sustained a tragic loss…The high ideals and the lofty standards set by Miss Snook served as a barometer by which we were to measure the future development of the library…It was her dogged determination and heroic tenacity that laid the foundation for our library of the future."[19]

Vera Snook, 1947

Photo courtesy of the
Arkansas Democrat-Gazette

1 Quote by President Roosevelt in "WPA Libraries Are Sources of Much Pleasure and Profit," *The Advocate [Fordyce, Arkansas]*, October 21, 1937.

2 Vera Snook Papers, University of Illinois at Urbana-Champaign, University Archives, University Library, Graduate School of Information and Library Sciences, Director's Alumni File, RS 18/1/42, Box 28. A copy of this file is now available as part of the CALS collection.

3 The 1927 American Library Directory reported nineteen municipal libraries in Arkansas. As the largest of these, the Little Rock Public Library reported 38,000 volumes, which still amounted to barely half a book each for Little Rock's population of 74,216. In her 1928 annual report, Snook referred to a report from the University of Arkansas that found that Arkansas had 27,000 more cars in the state than it had books in its public libraries. The Arkansas Free Library Service Bureau also reported that the amount appropriated for libraries in all of the state was less than the amount recommended as a minimum for the city of Little Rock alone.

4 In 1941, Eliza Atkins Gleason, the first African American to earn a PhD in library science, undertook an in-depth study of library service to black patrons in the South (see note 17). She questioned the logic of using poor circulation as a factor in determining funding for a library unit, especially when collections in the black libraries she studied were so often made up of old books cast off from the white library's collection.

5 *Arkansas Gazette*, May 4, 1934.

6 1937 annual report.

7 *Arkansas Democrat*, March 28, 1938.

8 United Community Funds and Councils of America, *The Little Rock Survey: A Four Weeks Study of Public and Private Social Work in Greater Little Rock, Arkansas, April 1939 by the Association of Community Chests and Councils, Inc.* (New York: Association of Community Chests and Councils, 1939).

9 Shirer later authored *The Rise and Fall of the Third Reich*.

10 Charlotte McWhorter, "Margaret Burkhead Has a Faculty for Keeping Busy," unidentified newspaper clipping, ca. 1952.

11 *Arkansas Gazette*, June 5, 1942.

12 According to the 1946 annual report, the record collection had grown to include 511 records by the end of that year.

13 The 1943 edition of *Who's Who in Library Service* listed the following librarians for the Little Rock Public Library: Sarah E. Large, Anna L. Russell, and Vera J. Snook. Sarah Large, a native of Denver, Colorado, had been reference librarian at the Little Rock Public Library since 1929. Anna Russell, an Arkansas native and a former teacher, became the assistant librarian at the Little Rock Public Library after completing a degree in library science in 1938.

14 *Arkansas Gazette*, May 1, 1947.

15 Smith served as librarian until the branch was closed in 1972. She then transferred to the main library and eventually retired from there.

16 Almeta Smith, who served as a branch manager and in various library departments, first worked as a page at the Ivey Branch during her high school years. An oral history interview with her about her service at the Ivey Branch is available at the Butler Center for Arkansas Studies.

17 Eliza Atkins Gleason, *The Southern Negro and the Public Library: A Study of the Government and Administration of Public Library Service to Negroes in the South* (Chicago, IL: University of Chicago Press, 1941). Gleason wrote analytically and dispassionately about each aspect of library service, including the legal requirements, and compared how service was applied in the white community versus the black community. Her work came at a time when such analysis was widely applied to establish the legal basis for black citizens to demand equal access and equal rights in many areas. Thus she set the stage for a gradual opening of public libraries in the South to the black community. Gleason pointed out that, in American law,

all local self-government stems from permission granted by the state; thus, she said, "The state is the ultimate source of the powers exercised by local library authorities attached to political subdivisions of the state." Gleason carried the point further by stating that library laws, as a function of state law, were subject to the "restraints of the Constitution," including the 14th Amendment requirement of due process and equal protection. Thus, she maintained, if the city provided a free public library for the white population, it was required to also provide a free public library for the black population.

18 Quoted in Rosebud Harris Tillman, "The History of Public Library Service to Negroes in Little Rock, Arkansas, 1917–1951" (MLS thesis, School of Library Service, Atlanta, GA, 1953).

19 *Arkansas Gazette*, March 2, 1948.

From Carnegie to Cyberspace: 100 Years at the Central Arkansas Library System

chapter five

THE BEGINNINGS OF COUNTY LIBRARIES IN ARKANSAS, 1923–1950

"A community without a library is a community whose soul is asleep."

PULASKI COUNTY LIBRARY ASSOCIATION, 1937[1]

At the same time the Little Rock Public Library was struggling to come into its own as a tax-supported institution, another library development was under way in the state—county libraries. To understand fully the history of the Central Arkansas Library System, the parallel stories of the libraries established to serve Pulaski and Perry counties must be told.

The work that came to fruition with the founding of county libraries in the 1930s had actually started a decade before. When librarian Beatrice Prall left the Little Rock Public Library, she went to work for the Arkansas Free Library Service Bureau (AFLSB), a state program established by the legislature in 1921 to encourage development of public libraries in Arkansas. The AFLSB received its first appropriation in 1923, which was intended to be used for the librarian's salary and for maintenance, not for books. The law establishing the bureau put it under the control of the Department of Education, aided by an advisory board made up of the state superintendent of education, the chairman of the library extension division of the Federation of Women's Clubs, the chairman of the library committee of the Arkansas Education Association, and the president of the Arkansas Library Association.

The AFLSB provided traveling libraries, as well as encouragement and advice, to communities that wanted to start their own public libraries. The traveling libraries provided by the organization Prall headed set the stage for county libraries.

Funding for County Libraries

The Arkansas legislature passed Act 244, the county library law, on March 24, 1927. This law allowed counties to establish and operate free county libraries and to appropriate tax money to support them. Under this law, the county's quorum court would appoint a six-person County Library Board. The county library would be located in the county seat and provide service throughout the county through branch libraries, deposit stations, and other means. Another option for county library boards under this law would be to contract with existing municipal libraries to provide service to the rural areas of the county.

Judge C. P. Newton appointed a library board for Pulaski County in 1927. The quorum court appropriated $7,500, and the county Board of Education appropriated $2,500, to establish a county library. Members of the board, however, could not agree on how to establish the library. Some members proposed housing the county library in a room of the courthouse; others wanted to enter into an agreement with the Little Rock Public Library. Because of the deadlock, no action was taken toward establishing the library, and the money was rescinded and used for other purposes.[2]

Although the new law opened the door for the creation of county libraries, it did not mandate them nor did it fund them. Creating a climate in which county governments were willing to approve and fund libraries became the goal of the Arkansas Federation of Women's Clubs and the American Legion Auxiliary. Their efforts were made possible by various New Deal funding efforts and by grants from the Rosenwald Fund.

The Rosenwald Fund, established by Julius Rosenwald, part owner of Sears, Roebuck, and Company, set up a program designed to extend library service into the counties in Southern states. Grants were based on the state providing a matching amount, beyond what it had already appropriated for library service. Arkansas was the first state to receive such a grant, which was administered through the Arkansas Free Library Service Bureau. Coupled with the required state match, the AFLSB had a budget of $7,550 for the 1930–1931 biennium.

The AFLSB, with help from the other organizations, used these funds to establish demonstration libraries. The organizers hoped that once people had access to books through the demonstration libraries, they would be more likely to pursue and support the extension of public library service into their communities. The Panhellenic Society of Little Rock took responsibility for the first demonstration library, which was opened in Roland, a rural community in northwest Pulaski County. This demonstration library operated from 1931 to 1932, after which it was moved to Jacksonville.

In 1933, Bessie Boehm Moore testified before a congressional committee in support of a bill to increase library funding. Moore, a former assistant school superintendent in Jefferson County in the late 1920s, used her innate political skills and worked tirelessly for the public library movement. During her testimony to the congressional committee, she noted that despite the progress being made, it would take another twenty-five years for all the counties in Arkansas to have libraries, and "we cannot afford to wait twenty-five years to have informed

Bessie Moore
Clipping courtesy of the *Arkansas Democrat-Gazette*

citizens who can act intelligently on the issues upon which they must pass judgment." The bill, which included funding for bookmobiles, passed.[3]

Adolphine Fletcher Terry (daughter of Adolphine Krause Fletcher, early library supporter), as chair of the library committee for the Arkansas American Legion Association, also led efforts for using the funds available through the New Deal programs and the Rosenwald Fund to promote libraries around the state. Perry County first enjoyed library service as one of the deposit stations established through the leadership of Terry during the 1930s.

In addition to providing a basic book collection and initial funding for a librarian, these efforts funded training for local librarians. Terry described the effect of this training in her diary: "On one occasion we invited all the librarians to the Little Rock Public Library to spend the day meeting each other and learning to be better librarians. About ninety came and I was amazed at the transformation. They were no longer poor people, earning a pittance to stay alive; they had become missionaries for books, for learning, for culture, for the future of their state. They knew it, and they were proud of their contribution to the development of Arkansas."[4]

Establishing the Pulaski County Library

In 1937, the state legislature appropriated $64,000 for county libraries to purchase books. In order to qualify for a share of the money,[5] the county was required to provide additional funding for operations. Not waiting for the quorum court to act this time, a citizens' group, the Pulaski County Library Association, presented a petition to the court requesting the matching appropriation required to qualify the county for a share of the state money. The court appropriated $5,000 for the county library in December 1937. Unfortunately, county revenue did not meet projections, and the appropriation could not be included in the 1938 budget. Judge J. G. Burlingame, in a determined effort to help create the county library, called for budget reductions across county departments and pledged that these savings of approximately $5,000 would go to the county library.

Burlingame appointed a new Pulaski County Library Board on January 11, 1938. The question of location was decided when State Librarian Alfred Rawlinson adamantly argued that having a separate facility would be wasteful. By February 1938, the Pulaski County Library was established in the LRPL building, and books were being selected for distribution. Books were chosen to meet the particular needs of the rural communities the library would serve—agriculture, prospective industries, health, adult education, recreation, and hobbies, as well as provide leisure reading.[6]

County libraries that received more than $8,000 of state aid were required to employ a graduate of an accredited library school. Lois Ranier, who had served as librarian at the College of Engineering at the University of Arkansas in Fayetteville, was appointed librarian on April 4, 1938, and assumed her new duties on May 1. On May 2, 1938, the *Arkansas Democrat* quoted Vera Snook as saying, "The county librarian is here and has the book situation well in hand."

Adolphine Fletcher Terry

Bookmobiles

The primary effort of the Pulaski County Library was to provide bookmobile service to areas outside the city of Little Rock. However, the funding received from the county was insufficient to fund salaries, operations, and a bookmobile. The Pulaski County Library Board began a fundraising effort to secure $2,500 to purchase and operate a bookmobile. The fundraisers asked that each child living in rural Pulaski County communities send a dime to help buy a bookmobile. The Greater Little Rock Library Association contributed $500, and the Home Demonstration Clubs gave $25. The board raised the rest of the money through public subscription.

Until a bookmobile could be secured, Ranier borrowed a car to use for community visits. She chose the community of Blue Hill for her first stop when service was initiated on May 19, 1938, because the school children in that community were the first to send in a per capita donation toward the purchase of a bookmobile. Within the first two weeks of operation, the rural library service distributed 2,054 books.

Side view of the bookmobile.

Children using the bookmobile.

The shiny green bookmobile cost approximately $1,200 and went into service on July 10, 1938. Ranier displayed the books behind glass panels that could be raised so that the public could browse and make selections.

In 1941, the county library purchased a new bookmobile; Gordon Bennett, the county librarian who succeeded Ranier, said the rural school children had sold bookmobile booster buttons to raise money for the new vehicle.

For the first time, the bookmobile would be going to African-American schools, using a special collection of 1,175 books, purchased in part with WPA funds. The collection delivered to one of those schools, in College Station, was advertised as the College Station Negro Branch of the Pulaski County Library.

The bookmobile also served the Jacksonville area, where in 1941 extensive wartime construction was under way. The Pulaski County Library, at the request of interested citizens in Jacksonville, was already considering a full-service branch in Jacksonville to accommodate the large number of users.

In 1944, the Pulaski County Library received a grant of $500 to provide service for African-American residents. Deposit stations in the black communities in Scott, Natural Steps, Roland, and Wampoo were established. These stations operated through the schools in the winter and through the Negro County Home Demonstration Clubs in the summer.

County librarian Lois Ranier (far left) and Foster Vineyard (in white hat) from the Greater Little Rock Library Association demonstrate the first Pulaski County Bookmobile.

Library Efforts in Perry County

While the funds available through the Arkansas Library Commission were jumpstarting the Pulaski County Library, smaller counties were struggling to realize their library dreams. The success of the deposit station in Perry County prompted the formation of the Perry County Library Association, and the citizens looked for ways to create a county library for this rural area, which had a population of 7,695 at the 1930 census. Because Perry County did not meet the 20,000 population threshold, it received little or no state assistance for a library.

The appropriations to the Arkansas Library Commission in 1941 and 1943, while not offering financial assistance to less-populated counties, did allow the state librarian to visit and provide advice to smaller counties. Members of the Perry County Library Association were convinced that they could offer limited service until state aid was available. After several years of effort, the county reached an agreement with Conway County in 1949 for the Conway County Library to extend services to neighboring Perry County. A panel truck was used to deliver books to deposit stations in outlying areas of both counties.[7]

The efforts of both the Pulaski and Perry county library supporters were the first steps toward bringing library service to the rural areas of both counties. These efforts continued for the next three decades—until the merger with the Little Rock Public Library.

1 *Arkansas Democrat* clipping, December 11, 1937, Library Scrapbook 1937–1940, Number 2.

2 D. T. Henderson, Pulaski County school superintendent, who was a member of the Pulaski County Library Board, related this story in an article by William Johnson in the *Arkansas Democrat*, September 21, 1930. Pulaski County was not alone in failing to step through the door opened to library service through the 1927 law. When this article was written, the only county that had a functioning county library was Jefferson County, and that was the work of Bessie Boehm Moore, then Jefferson County school supervisor and later a national library leader.

3 George and Mildred Fersh, *Bessie Moore, A Biography* (Little Rock: August House, 1986).

4 Quoted in Stephanie M. Bayless, "A Southern Paradox: The Social Activism of Adolphine Fletcher Terry" (MA thesis, University of Arkansas at Little Rock, 2008).

5 The amount available to each county was based on the cost of the books purchased under state supervision. The appropriation was based on rural white population at a rate of 25 books for each 100 people.

6 Both the *Arkansas Democrat* and the *Arkansas Gazette* carried frequent articles during late 1937 and early 1938 about the development of the new Pulaski County Library. Indeed, throughout the history of library service in Arkansas, the local media have given the organization strong support, including regularly publishing book reviews and listings of new offerings at the library.

7 Gladys McNeil, "History of the Library in Arkansas" (Master's thesis, University of Mississippi, 1957).

chapter six

POST WORLD WAR II THROUGH 1974

"If this nation is to be wise as well as strong, if we are to achieve our destiny, then we need more new ideas for more wise men reading more good books in more public libraries. These libraries should be open to all."

SENATOR JOHN F. KENNEDY, OCTOBER 1960

After the death of Vera Snook, Catherine Chew became the acting librarian. The board appointed her to the permanent librarian position on November 10, 1948. Chew had joined the LRPL staff in 1929 as the children's librarian, but

Catherine Chew
Clipping courtesy of the
Arkansas Democrat-Gazette

she left that position to become the Pulaski County librarian. In 1946, she rejoined the LRPL as the reference librarian, and it was from that position that she ascended to head the library.

Friends and admirers of Vera Snook donated money to create a memorial to the indomitable librarian. The staff converted the auditorium into the Vera Snook Memorial Room, which was furnished with a turquoise velvet curtain, two mahogany Chippendale chairs, a matching mahogany reading stand, a solid brass candlestick lamp, an eighteenth-century inlaid mahogany table, and a portrait of Snook painted by Little Rock artist Adrian Brewer.

The demand for library services continued to grow, and the Little Rock Public Library continued to need more space and resources. The library that had opened in February 1910 with 2,160 books on the shelves had a collection totaling 103,544

The Vera Snook Memorial Room.
Photo courtesy of the *Arkansas Democrat-Gazette*

items at the end of 1948; the number of registered borrowers had grown from 1,146 the first year to 39,383 in 1948.

This period was marked by several major initiatives, most notably the desegregation of the LRPL and the construction of a new library building.

Desegregation of the Little Rock Public Library

Georg Iggers, a professor at Philander Smith College, began teaching at the college in the fall of 1950. He quickly became concerned about the inadequate library facilities available to his students at the college. Although the college had a library, it was small and did not have the books his students needed. The limited collection at the Colored Branch was divided between the adult and children's sections. Although patrons of the Colored Branch could theoretically borrow books from the main library, they had no idea what books were available because no catalog of the holdings of the main library existed at the branch.

Iggers wrote a letter to the editor of the *Arkansas Gazette*, published on November 3, 1950. He expressed not only his dismay at the inadequacy of resources available for students but also his concern about the probable illegality of restricting library service at the main library to whites only: "Library service in the city is not equal and cannot be equal as long a separate branch is maintained."

Board of Trustees' meeting minutes from 1950 show that the question of library access for African Americans had been discussed before Iggers's letter was published. In March of that year, the board discussed "a policy of lending books to Negroes and of allowing Negroes access to reference materials in the Main Library." They decided at that time to continue the current policy of lending books from the branch but agreed that "exceptions could be made at the

Prior to 1951, the Main Library's policy of whites only made the bulk of the library's research materials unavailable to African-American students.

Photo courtesy of the *Arkansas Democrat-Gazette*

From Carnegie to Cyberspace: 100 Years at the Central Arkansas Library System

discretion of the librarians; and that access to the reference collection of the Main Library be given also at the discretion of the librarians."

The publication of Iggers's letter brought the question to the attention of the public and prepared the community for the board's decision to open the main library to meet the needs of the students. In December, the board discussed the question again but deferred a decision while the staff talked to leaders in the black community regarding their recommendations. The resolution adopted by the trustees at their January 10, 1951, meeting provided that "the adult department of the main library be open to Negroes beginning with students of the seventh grade and to all negroes over the age of sixteen" and that "Negroes be required to make application for a library card in the same manner as white patrons."[1]

The board positioned its decision as a practical matter, noting that the main library contained reference books and periodicals needed for research that would be too expensive to duplicate in the branch.

The board cited crowded conditions as the reason for not extending full access at the main library—especially in the children's department, which would limit its ability to offer children's programming—and also maintained that most of the black schools and homes were located closer to the branch than to the main library.[2]

At the same time African-American patrons were given this limited access to the main library, the branch library was still referred to in library records as the Colored Branch. On June 2, 1951, the branch became the namesake of Helen Booker Ivey, the former principal of Capitol Hill Elementary School. Ivey, who died in June 1946, was the daughter of Dr. Joseph Booker, the first president of Arkansas Baptist College. The Delta Sigma Theta sorority chapter had put forth the proposal to name the branch after Ivey. The chapter had established the children's book collection in her name after her death, and the members made yearly contributions to it.

Attorney J. R. Booker, representing the Booker family; Mrs. T. Tatum, chairperson of the dedication committee; Sue Williams, president of the local Delta Sigma Theta chapter; and Adolphine Terry, representing the LRPL Board of Trustees, at the Helen Booker Ivey Branch dedication.

Clipping courtesy of the *Arkansas Democrat-Gazette*

Desegregation of the main library did not minimize the interest in or the need for full library service in the black community. Continued growth in circulation at the Ivey Branch showed the ongoing need for local access to library service. Circulation at the branch increased by about 5,000 in 1951, and 200 new registered users were added at the branch. This suggests that the most robust use of the branch was by children (who were not granted access to the main library) and recreational readers. Another need filled at the branch rather than the main library was the availability of books and materials by and about African Americans.

The Ivey Branch remained the primary library for the black community. Public school students used the Ivey Branch as a resource, and librarian Louise Smith made sure their needs were met. Students at Gibbs Elementary School regularly studied black history—researching, writing papers, and presenting reports. Melrita Bonner, who went to the library almost weekly as a child, noted that she was not aware until she was an adult that there was any other library in Little Rock,[3] and Marion Woods related, "When I turned six years old my father took everyone in the family to the African American Library on 16th Street to get a library card. He said it would be the most important card I would ever carry in my purse."[4]

The county library bookmobile service continued to make books available to underserved communities. The longest trip the bookmobile made in 1948, for example, was 78 miles round trip to the Little Italy community. The arrival of the bookmobile was a big event in the communities; often, there would be such a crowd that one person would read to the children while they waited to get on the bookmobile.

The limited desegregation of the LRPL also opened the door for changes in the bookmobile's service. Prior to the expansion of services, bookmobiles serving Pulaski County schools carried from one to three boxes of books in the back "for colored people." While plans for a new bookmobile included "complete space on one side for colored use," after the board's decision, Pulaski County librarian Mary Sue Shepherd reported that "colored and white receive the same service jointly."[5]

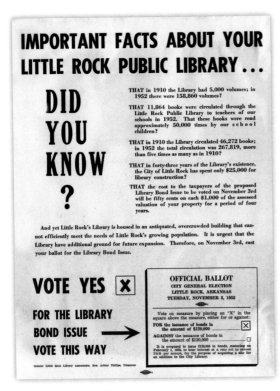

The Greater Little Rock Library Association helped campaign for the library bond issue by making the public more aware of the library's needs.

New Era, New Challenges

In 1953, the LRPL Board asked the city council to present a bond issue for $800,000 to the people, which would allow for the purchase of property as well as the construction of a new building. The city council refused that request but did agree to ask for $120,000 to purchase the lots on the south end of the block between 7th and 8th streets on the west side of Louisiana.[6]

Lack of space and financial resources created many problems that left the library below national standards. June Dwellingham, a native of Little Rock and a student at the Drexel Institute of Technology School of Library Science in Philadelphia, undertook a survey of the LRPL as her master's thesis in 1954.[7] This evaluation measured the library against the Post-War Standards for Public Libraries developed by the American Library Association (ALA) in 1943.

The LRPL met some of the ALA standards; for instance, the location was ideal because it was close to businesses and shopping areas. The governance and administrative arrangements also followed closely the ALA's recommendations: The Board of Trustees was appointed by the mayor and the city council, and, as Vera Snook had wished for years before, they were chosen "with reference for their fitness for such an office." The trustees in turn functioned as "the legislative body for the library," setting policy and leaving the librarian to carry it out.

By other measurements, however, the library fell far short of the ALA mark. Against the recommended budget provision and expenditure of $1.50 per capita, Little Rock spent less than half of that—69.9 cents in 1953. The standards required 1.75 books per capita, and the library's collection was only 1.19 books per capita.

In the introduction to her study, Dwellingham repeated what was often observed about the LRPL: the staff demonstrated a "warm and congenial attitude" that contributed dramatically to the success of their services. She remarked on the commitment to provide the best possible service in spite of limited funding. Despite their relatively low salaries, the staff had training in library service; only the circulation librarian lacked such training, and she had fifteen years of library experience.[8]

Catherine Chew's health declined during this period, and she worked only part time. Margaret Burkhead assumed more and more of Chew's duties and succeeded Chew in 1957 to become the first person to hold the title "director" at the LRPL.

Margaret Burkhead

Cooperative programs continued to expand the reach of the LRPL beyond its inadequate facilities. For example, the Panhellenic Association, an organization made up of alumnae of various sororities, opened a children's library at 2009 North Van Buren in 1955. The LRPL and the Arkansas State Library Commission each gave them 500 books to start the library. The organizers chose the Heights location because it was more convenient for children than the downtown library.

In the summer of 1956, the LRPL worked with the Panhellenic Association to create a summer reading club at the children's library in the Heights.[9] Although it was not officially part of the LRPL, the children's library circulation statistics were included in the library's annual reports because the library provided books for its collection and cooperated with the summer reading program.

Construction and Grand Opening

The summer of 1955 marked a reactivation of the Greater Little Rock Library Association—under the new name the "Friends of the Library." In November, plans were made to expand the group, which had membership dues of $2 per year. Fred K. Darragh Jr. served as president of the newly reorganized group. The Friends once again geared up to raise public awareness of the library's needs.

Although the library was governed by its own Board of Trustees, it was part of the city, so city voters had to approve the borrowing of funds for a new building. Construction had to be paid for with a bond issue because the library taxes were limited by the state constitution to one mill, and that money could be spent only for operations. Supporters of expanding the library moved forward with plans to incorporate portions of the existing library building into a new one, and preliminary plans were ready by the fall of 1956 with an estimated cost of nearly $1.3 million. The bond issue for "construction and remodeling of the present building," would be paid for by continuing a level of taxation that would otherwise have expired in 1957, which meant that the question could go to the voters with the promise that passage would not result in an increase in their property taxes.

Voters approved the proposal, but multiple delays held up construction on the building, which was not complete until late in 1963. One of the delays involved the allowed interest rate on the bonds approved to fund the construction. Because the average rate available at the time was higher than was allowed to be offered on these bonds, no one made a bid for the bonds when they were first offered for sale.

The library plaza stood
on the location of the
original Carnegie building.

The question of the bond issue was taken to the voters again in November 1957, with the understanding that the city could set the rate at whatever was needed to ensure a sale. By the time the bonds sold in January 1958, the rate ended up being lower than the initial 3.25 percent offered.

The plan to replace the existing library had grown out of a national trend toward revitalizing urban areas. Following the passage of the Housing Act of 1954, the federal government had made funds available for its urban renewal program. In 1959, the government extended its urban renewal program to aid in redeveloping downtown areas.

Little Rock formed the Central Little Rock Urban Renewal Project in 1962 and proposed a major undertaking that would encompass both the central business district and adjacent residential areas. This project was the first of its kind to be approved by the Federal Urban Renewal Administration.

This spirit of urban renewal bled over into the library's plans, which were presented to the public as an addition to the existing library. In actuality, a completely new building was constructed with the north end encompassing the south reading room of the original Carnegie building. The rest of the original building was then torn down.[10]

In 1959, in preparation for the move to the new building, the staff undertook the first book weeding in the history of the library system, withdrawing almost 7,000 books.

Little Rock native Donald Harington, in his 1965 debut novel *The Cherry Pit*, described the old and the new buildings standing side by side, and also hinted at the role the Little Rock Public Library played in Harington's own early years. The novel's main character, Clifford Stone, who bears a strong resemblance to the young Harington, returned to his hometown of Little Rock, where he visited "the public library, its waffled modern façade gone up like a masonry carapace around the homely old Carnegie edifice which…had been my favorite refuge in a youth of applied cultivation of my mind and body." [11]

In May 1963, construction on the new building was complete enough to allow library service to begin in the building. When the move was complete, the remains of the original building were demolished to make room for a garden plaza, parking for staff, and a garage for bookmobiles.

The Friends of the Library raised the last $9,000 needed for the construction of a north entrance to the library and the garden and plaza surrounding it. The balance was paid by the Housing Authority for this urban renewal project. A zoning variance also had to be obtained from the city to allow for fewer parking spaces than otherwise required for a facility such as a library.

The formal opening of the building was not held until the entire project was completed in 1964. At the dedication of the plaza, Little Rock mayor Martin Borchert lauded the library for its role in supporting renewal of the city's downtown area. "To maintain a viable downtown area…a city must do more than build a collection of steel, concrete and brick. It must…be convenient, interesting, and most of all, attractive….The Library Plaza will be an inspiration to other concerns as they contemplate new construction in downtown Little Rock."

Bessie Moore also spoke at this dedication event, advocating a constitutional amendment that would raise the one-mill tax limit. She said the tax "wasn't adequate then, and it's even less adequate now." Another twenty-five years would pass, however, before Moore's recommendation would be heeded.

The expansion allowed greater access for all patrons, and, gradually, all the services, including story time and other public programming, were opened to all members of the community. The Ivey Branch remained open, however, and served as an important gathering place for the community surrounding it—especially for the students who benefited from Louise Smith's training, encouragement, and discipline.

With more space available for books, the librarians also turned their attention to expanding the collection. The Library Services and Construction Act, which passed in 1964, provided funds for some expansion of library services in Little Rock.[12] In 1965, the library's book budget increased by $25,000 as a result of funds available through this federal program. Approximately 40 percent of the library's book purchases for the next few years were made with federal funds.

The local history collection grew over the years, mostly through gifts. The new building included not only the Arkansas Room that had been established in the 1930s but also a genealogy desk. The library owned a substantial genealogy book collection, which had grown over the years through frequent contributions from the local chapter of the Daughters of the American Revolution. These books were part of the reference section and could not be checked out.

Although access to the Arkansas Room required a patron to sign in, no one oversaw the use of the collection. This changed in 1967 after an inventory revealed that several valuable books, some of which were irreplaceable, were missing. At that time, the library hired Mrs. Joe Hale as genealogy custodian

MOVING THE LIBRARY

The city and the county library collections totaled 154,000 books, which not only had to be moved but also had to be kept in the same order during the move.

The Terminal Warehouse Company, which had experience moving libraries, undertook the task, using specially constructed wooden dollies and ramps built between the old building and the new building; this same system of maintaining the order of books continues to be used by the library today. S. J. "Stony" Beauchamp Jr., the moving company official in charge of the transfer, in describing the care and the pride that his company took in the move, said, "I told my men they couldn't drop a book and to treat all of the books as priceless treasures." The Terminal Warehouse Company once used one of the historic buildings now incorporated into the Arkansas Studies Institute as warehouse space.

to assist genealogy librarian Mrs. E. V. Jackson. A lack of funding, however, allowed the room to be open only from 9:00 a.m. to 1:00 p.m. Tuesday through Saturday. As a result of Hale's work with patrons, use of the genealogy collection increased.

Censorship and Privacy

The Arkansas Library Association adopted a resolution in 1950 affirming its commitment to the library as an agent of intellectual freedom: "We reaffirm and state our steadfast belief in freedom of expression, freedom of acquisition for library collections, and freedom of access to libraries by all people, because these are irreducible factors of a free society." This commitment was tested in April 1960 when the Little Rock Censor Board[13] banned the book *Return to Peyton Place.* The public library declined to remove the book from its shelves, saying that "the book was available under their 'rental book' system but no public money was used in purchasing the book…The censor board has nothing to do with the public library...We would not want to remove the book from the library because that would be censoring reading, and we don't want to do that."[14]

Rev. Guy Wilson, chairman of the Little Rock Censor Board's committee on publications, defended the group's actions in that and other incidents of banning books: "It is not the wishes of the board to prohibit mature persons from reading books,...[but] to protect the innocent ones—those who could be led into delinquency."

The public library's commitment to providing the fullest possible spectrum of information and protecting the First Amendment rights of its patrons often puts it at odds with those who find some of the holdings objectionable. The institution maintains a similar commitment to protecting its patrons' privacy. Not long after Alice Gray replaced Margaret Burkhead as director, she had to address the question of patron privacy.

Reports came out in July 1970 that Treasury Department investigators had approached libraries in several cities asking for information on who had checked out books on explosives or guerrilla warfare. The reports drew sharp criticism from library organizations, from political leaders, and from members of the library community.

Gray, responding to questions about how such inquiries would be handled locally, stated her belief that patrons have the right and the freedom to read whatever they want to. She reported that, for at least the previous twenty years, books on such subjects had been kept at the desk and could not be checked out to children without a note from their parents. The library's Board of Trustees responded to the questions raised by adopting a resolution establishing the policy that information on library patrons would not be given out.

Reaching Out beyond Downtown

Inadequate parking had been a critical issue for the library for several years, especially with the construction of the new Southwestern Bell building opposite the library on the Louisiana Street side, which blocked most of the street parking. In 1970, proceeds from the Emmet Morris Memorial Fund were used to purchase the parking lot on the southwest corner of 8th and Louisiana; the greater availability of parking contributed to a significant increase in circulation for the year.

Little Rock had grown to include residential areas west and southwest of the central city area. In addition to bookmobile service provided by the county library, the LRPL acquired a bookmobile in 1971 through the Arkansas Library Commission, using Library Services and Construction Act funds. Called the Traveling Branch, the thirty-five-foot-long, blue and yellow bookmobile could hold 5,000 books. This bookmobile served outlying areas of the city, including schools and shopping centers.

BANNING LIBRARY MATERIALS

The American Library Association (ALA) gathers statistics on books that have been challenged in the public library. Included among the lists of books most challenged during the past decade are:

- *The Adventures of Huckleberry Finn* by Mark Twain
- *As I Lay Dying* by William Faulkner
- *The Catcher in the Rye* by J. D. Salinger
- Harry Potter series by J. K. Rowling
- *The Color Purple* by Alice Walker
- *The Grapes of Wrath* by John Steinbeck
- *I Know Why the Caged Bird Sings* by Maya Angelou

At CALS, once an item has been formally challenged, the director appoints a committee to review the material, but the final decision rests with the director. During Bobby Roberts's tenure as director, only one book (*Borat: Touristic Guidings to Glorious Nation of Kazakhstan*) and one video (*Wicked Lake*) have been removed from the collection (although *Borat* was removed only from the branches). Roberts says he and the committee members consider the following criteria:

- Does the item fall outside the scope of the library's selection policy, which requires it to have materials for a wide variety of readers?
- Does the item violate the library's standards of community decency?
- Is the item properly classified?

With the bookmobile service in place, the Board of Trustees decided at its June 1972 meeting to close the Ivey Branch at the end of that year and provide bookmobile service to the area in its place.

A smaller vehicle called the Rarin'-to-Read Mobile, which began service in 1972, made stops at daycare centers and community agencies that served the needs of children, such as the Elizabeth Mitchell Children's Center. The goal of the service was to introduce reading to children who otherwise would not come to the library, presenting it in a way that would be fun. One outgrowth of this service was an increase in the number of centers bringing their children to the downtown library for the Tuesday and Saturday pre-school programs.

The library printed this postcard with a photo of the bookmobile on the front and the schedule of services on the back to distribute in the community.

Bookmobile patrons also participated in the library's summer reading club, supported at the time by the McDonald's fast-food restaurant. Patricia Egeston, the bookmobile's librarian, reported that fifty children completed the required number of books to earn the reward of a hamburger and french fries in 1976, and 250 won the prize in 1977.

The cooperative agreement with the Panhellenic Children's Library continued to provide an opportunity to allow easier access to books. In 1973, the Children's Library moved to 2312 Durwood Road in a space donated by St. Michael's Episcopal Church. At that time, the Children's Library had a collection of approximately 9,000 books, 6,000 of them on loan from the Little Rock Public Library and the Arkansas Library Commission.

In 1973, the library had set up a reading room service at the East Little Rock Community Center, located at 2500 East 6th Street. Initially funded with Model City funds, the project eventually became the responsibility of the Little Rock Public Library. Sometimes referred to as the East Little Rock Branch Library, this location was staffed on a part-time basis.

The Board of Trustees also pursued other means to provide library service to the growing city. They hired library consultant Gretchen Schenk, who had earlier done a study of library service in the state for the Library Commission, to study needs and provide recommendations. Schenk was especially known for her work with library extension services. Her study included both the Little Rock Public Library and the Pulaski–Perry County Regional Library. She made recommendations that led to discussions in 1974 for combining the two systems. Also, at the request of the Board of Trustees, Metroplan studied the need for library service to the growing suburban areas and made recommendations for the locations of branch libraries.[15]

The Board of Trustees purchased a building at H and Buchanan streets in April 1974. The decision to establish a branch in west Little Rock and to plan service in southwest Little Rock marked the beginning of a commitment to expansion that continues today. The John Gould Fletcher Library opened in 1974 to provide service that could no longer be provided by the Main Library.

Pulaski and Perry County Libraries

During these years, the Pulaski County Library also experienced growth and expansion. Staffed by one trained librarian, three full-time helpers, and three part-time helpers, it continued to rent space in the basement of the Main Library. In 1950, the citizens of rural Pulaski County voted for a one-mill county tax to support the library, which gave it the same type of dedicated tax support that the Little Rock Public Library received.

Funds from the tax allowed the Pulaski County Library to replace the bookmobile that had been in use since 1938. The new bookmobile cost $9,500, increased the book capacity from 1,200 to 2,300 volumes, and was heated in the winter and electrically fanned in the summer.

In September 1960, Bessie Moore approached the Pulaski County Library Board to propose that the Pulaski County Library consider working with Perry County on library service. Following a series of meetings and discussions, the Perry County Library Board asked the Pulaski County Library Board to approve regional library service. The Pulaski–Perry County Library System came into being during the fall of 1961, initially under the direction of the Pulaski County Board of Trustees. The Perry County Branch of the new system opened on December 3, 1961, in a concrete-block structure on the courthouse square in the county seat, Perryville.

Throughout these years, county library service was mainly by means of bookmobiles. According to a 1961 article in the *Arkansas Gazette*, the county library's 38,000-volume collection included books in Italian (for some of the older residents of Little Italy, who did not read English) and in Polish (for Polish-speaking inhabitants of Marche and Blue Hill). The bookmobile, which carried 2,300 books at a time, as well as filmstrips and other resources, visited each rural service area every three weeks.[16]

Increased usage led to the call for full-service branch libraries in some areas. The Pulaski County Library, at the request of local citizens, opened a branch in Jacksonville in 1959; in 1973, the Pulaski–Perry County Regional Library opened a branch in Sherwood.

Negotiations continued throughout 1974 on the proposal to merge the Pulaski–Perry County Regional Library and the Little Rock Public Library. The boards of both organizations had approved the proposal by April 1974. In subsequent months, the mayor of Little Rock and the county judges of Pulaski and Perry counties also approved the merger. At that point, what had been parallel histories with minor overlap now became a unified story of the Central Arkansas Library System.

1 Another decision was made at the same Board of Trustees meeting: "The Board approved the installation of a lavatory in the small room adjoining the County stack room, cost not to exceed $100.00." While the minutes do not give the reason for making that decision at that exact time, the customs of the day suggest that it was to accommodate the black patrons who would now be using the building.

2 June H. Dwellingham, "A General Survey of the Little Rock (Arkansas) Public Library" (MLS thesis, Drexel Institute of Technology School of Library Science, 1954).

3 Interview with Melrita Bonner, available at the Butler Center for Arkansas Studies.

4 Taken from a 2009 patron survey conducted for this book.

5 Rosebud Harris Tillman, "The History of Public Library Service to Negroes in Little Rock, Arkansas, 1917–1951" (MLS thesis, School of Library Service, Atlanta, GA, 1953).

6 Dwellingham, "A General Survey of the Little Rock (Arkansas) Public Library."

7 Dwellingham, "A General Survey of the Little Rock (Arkansas) Public Library"; Dwellingham's major source of information was interviews with the head librarian and the branch librarian. She said, "The library has no published reports, and there was a scarcity of printed information concerning it." Library employees who participated in her research were Librarian Catherine T. Chew, Executive Secretary Margaret Burkhead, and also Mrs. L. W. Smith (Louise), librarian of the Ivey Branch. Research was done between December 21, 1953, and January 2, 1954. The author had in the past worked for the Little Rock Public Library. Writing in the third person, she said, "[The author] has experienced as a reader the many ways in which such a library [in a small city] can open up broader cultural and educational horizons," vii.

8 Dwellingham, "A General Survey of the Little Rock (Arkansas) Public Library."

9 *Arkansas Gazette*, May 27, 1956. After the opening of the Fletcher Branch, this collection was incorporated into the Little Rock Public Library. The Fletcher Branch, which opened in 1974 near where the children's library had been, still maintains a relationship with the Panhellenic Association and cooperates with it on special projects (Kate Matthews, Fletcher Branch manager, September 30, 2008, interview).

10 The rush toward urban renewal birthed another movement—historic preservation. The Quapaw Quarter area of Little Rock was designated as a historic residential area in an effort to preserve the architectural history of that area. Unfortunately, the historic preservation movement arrived too late to save the Little Rock Public Library building.

11 Donald Harington, *The Cherry Pit* (1956) (New York: Mariner Books/Harcourt, 1989), 56. Harington, who taught at the University of Arkansas in Fayetteville, went on to write more than fifteen books and numerous articles. He is the winner of several literary awards, as well as the 2006 Lifetime Achievement Award in Southern Literature from the *Oxford American* magazine.

12 The Library Services and Construction Act, developed during John F. Kennedy's presidency, made federal funding available for local libraries. The bill was coming to a vote in the Senate on November 22, 1963. Although it generally had strong support, opposition to the construction portions of it would have emerged if the process had not been interrupted by President Kennedy's assassination. When the Senate resumed after the funeral, the bill was seen as a memorial to the slain president. In January 1964, it passed the Senate 89-7 and also passed dramatically in the House.

13 First established in 1908, the Little Rock Censor Board was active at various times in attempting to censor public performances, movies, and publications. Made up of fifteen members appointed by city aldermen, the board administered censorship rules that had been approved by the Little Rock City Board of Directors. Although it did not have police powers, it could make a determination to ban books, meaning that certain books could not be sold at bookstores or on newsstands in Little Rock. According to those rules, any three members of the board could declare any publication banned without prior notice. Once the Little Rock Censor Board declared something banned, it was up to the police department to enforce the decision.

14 "Library Won't Drop Book Censored Here," *Arkansas Democrat*, April 9, 1960, p. 1; Little Rock Censor Board Minutes, April 7, 1960. Copy in the personal collection of Timothy G. Nutt.

15 Metroplan is a regional planning organization founded in 1955. Since 1972, it has been the Metropolitan Planning Organization, charged with providing planning and technical assistance to local and state government groups. With local organizations, it helps determine federal funding priorities.

16 *Arkansas Gazette*, January 22, 1961.

chapter seven

THE EARLY YEARS OF CALS, 1975–1989

"It is the belief of the library Boards that this consolidation will not weaken the concept of the small community library. Instead, it will strengthen and offer greatly expanded resources and services to library users."

JOINT STATEMENT OF THE LITTLE ROCK PUBLIC LIBRARY BOARD AND THE PULASKI–PERRY REGIONAL LIBRARY BOARD, FEBRUARY, 1975

Effective February 1975, the Little Rock Public Library and Pulaski–Perry Regional Library merged, and the Central Arkansas Library System (CALS) was born. The operating document for the merged organization was the Interlocal Government Cooperation Agreement, made between the county and municipal bodies that joined the new system. In this document, with the approval of state law, each of the political jurisdictions ceded to the library system the functions that allowed it to establish and maintain public libraries.[1]

The creation of the library system brought new opportunities and new challenges to the library staff. Alice Gray worked toward making all the parts come together into a cohesive system, but the lack of financial resources continued to impede growth.

OCLC Revolutionizes the Library

During this period, CALS entered the electronic age and took the first step toward automating the libraries. The Library of Congress had ushered in the electronic age for libraries across the country when it converted its bibliographic records into the MARC (machine readable cards) system in 1967. MARC records put standardized data into encoded language that allowed librarians to retrieve information described in standardized language. In Ohio, the OCLC (Ohio College Library Center) consortia joined fifty-four Ohio colleges into a network that used the Library of Congress's MARC records.[2]

The OCLC network revolutionized the cataloging process.

The OCLC network opened to libraries around the country via the nascent Internet. By the time CALS joined the network in 1975, more than 600 libraries around the country subscribed to OCLC. Prior to OCLC, each library had to create catalogue records from scratch, a fairly complex procedure that involved a good bit of research before a book could be put into circulation. Members of the OCLC network could use the computer to see if another institution had already done the due diligence research and created a record. If so, the member library could just copy that record. The shared record information significantly simplified the cataloguers' jobs and dramatically shortened the time needed to make books available. James Allen, librarian at the University of Arkansas at Little Rock (UALR), estimated that the cost of cataloguing new books by hand was $4.57 per book, and that OCLC would cut that cost to approximately $2.75.[3]

New Branch and New Leadership

Library patron (and future Pulaski County librarian) Mary Sue Shepherd recalled the first time library service came to the rural community where she lived, in the form of a bookmobile driven by Little Rock librarian Lois Green. "The first time the bus came to Mabelvale, so many people wanted to get on it that Mrs. Green asked me to sit on the steps of the high school and read to the children just to keep them busy until there was room for them to get to the books."[4]

By 1976, population growth in the rural Pulaski County area overwhelmed the bookmobile's ability to provide adequate service. In July of that year, the LRPL arranged for a storefront operation inside the Southwest Mall, located at the corner of Interstate 30 and Geyer Springs Road. During the first week of business, the branch issued 741 new library cards.

After Gray's death in May 1978, the board hired Rosemary Martin as director. Martin joined the system in December 1978. Prior to joining CALS, she had served as a zone manager for the Dallas Public Library in Texas from 1977 through late 1978. In Dallas, she directed six branch libraries serving a population of 262,600 with a combined collection of 456,526 volumes. At that time, the entire Central Arkansas Library System contained approximately 436,000 volumes and served a population of approximately 300,000.

CALS trustee Nell Henry, Governor Dale Bumpers, Rosemary Martin, and David Macksam.

From Carnegie to Cyberspace: 100 Years at the Central Arkansas Library System

Culture Clash

Rosemary Martin's management style differed greatly from Alice Gray's. Whereas Gray—who had started at the library as a page and worked her way up through the system—firmly believed in viewing the library staff as family, Martin viewed the staff members as replaceable employees. She strongly encouraged many of the older ladies who had been with the library for many years to retire, including Ida Mae Hagin, who had been the children's librarian for forty-three years and was much beloved in the community.[5]

In 1979, Martin brought in David Macksam, a branch librarian at Enoch Pratt Free Library in Baltimore, Maryland, to serve as head of extension services, which encompassed responsibility for the branch libraries and the bookmobile service. By the end of that year, Martin had decided to increase his responsibilities so that he could serve as her assistant director. Macksam quickly became the administrative point person for the library's staff, who rarely saw Martin.

Martin seemed naïve about the role politics played in the big picture of the library. She rarely appeared in public on behalf of the library; nor did she seem to be interested in building relationships with the "movers and shakers" who could have helped the library progress during this period.

Larrie Ohlemeyer (now Larrie Thompson), who joined CALS in 1987 as administrative assistant, offers some insight into Martin's mindset. She said, "Rosemary Martin told me almost straight off when I joined the library that she had selected CALS to be her final job—that she was looking for a place where she could relax and not have to put forth a whole lot of energy…She was not interested in being a spokesperson for the library."

Ida Mae Hagin with Charlotte Curlee, Ethalena Holdon, and Paul Frith in 1952. Hagin had been the children's librarian since the 1930s.
Photo courtesy of the *Arkansas Democrat-Gazette*

The Board of Trustees, however, had a much more high-energy approach in mind. Trustee Fred Darragh in particular was frustrated with Martin, and he concluded that she was not a good match with the board's vision for the library.

In November 1980, the Board of Trustees, under the leadership of its chairman Jo Ann Newell, undertook a two-year evaluation and planning process. The planning process was based on a handbook titled *A Planning Process for Public Libraries*, published in 1980 by the Public Library Association (PLA), a division of the American Library Association (ALA). It was designed to guide libraries and library systems in a study of local conditions to determine specific needs and set goals to meet those needs. FOCAL, Metroplan, and the Winthrop Rockefeller Foundation, along with other groups, supported and helped implement the effort.

To begin the study, the board formed a group called the Library System Planning Committee. Using the PLA book as a guide, they discussed ways the library could improve service while at the same time staying within its limited budget. The committee comprised twenty community leaders and residents from throughout Pulaski and Perry counties, chosen not because they were library experts, but because they were interested in library improvement. Jason Rouby, executive director of Metroplan and a member of the FOCAL board, chaired the committee. The study made use of resources available through Metroplan and through the Center for Urban and Governmental Affairs at the University of Arkansas at Little Rock.

The study report, *CALS' Future: A Matter of Public Priority*, presented to the Board of Trustees in November 1982, contained a thorough analysis of the communities CALS served, as well as an analysis of the system itself, seen through the eyes of staff members and patrons. Specific recommendations focused on three areas: Services and Programs, Collections, and Facilities. Underlying all of the recommendations was the need for increased funding.[6]

Financial Setbacks

Library funding, always difficult because of the one-mill cap on allowed library tax rates, suffered a severe setback in the first half of the 1980s. A 1979 Arkansas Supreme Court ruling required the reassessment of all property in the state for tax purposes. To help alleviate what many anticipated would be unmanageable property tax increases on the new and higher assessments, Constitutional Amendment 59 was proposed and passed in 1980. This measure rolled back millage rates, with the intent that no property owner would encounter more than a ten percent increase in actual taxes. Designers of the amendment intended that no state agency would actually lose funds but instead would remain generally even. But there were unintended consequences: Libraries already collecting the full one-mill tax had their rates cut, in some cases very drastically.[7]

Even if the full rates had been in place around the state, Arkansas would have a long way to go to meet recommended standards. The state was in last place in per capita library funding; the national per capita average was $10.73, compared to the Arkansas average of $3.42.

In 1982, the Arkansas Library Association attempted to get a constitutional amendment on the ballot for the fall election to lift the one-mill cap, using a statewide petition to do it. To get an amendment on the ballot by petition, the libraries had to secure a certain number of signatures from a certain number of counties to ensure that the initiative had support from across the state. Because it was the largest library system in the state and located in the capital, statewide efforts depended heavily on the initiative and leadership of the trustees and staff at CALS. Participation in the signature drive was meager in many of the counties, and the effort fell 40,000 short of the 127,000 signatures needed.

The CALS Board of Trustees members, at their regular meeting in July 1986, discussed ways to deal with an immediate, severe funding shortfall. They were faced with either cutting expenses by $45,000 to finish out the year, or finding other sources of income to make up the difference. Budgets for buying books and subscriptions were cut, and they instituted a charge of twenty-five cents for reserving a book. The board discussed closing on Sundays for the rest of the year, instead of resuming Sunday hours in September, as was the custom. As the board faced these decisions, Director Martin acknowledged her error in the budgeting process for the year and took responsibility for not coming to the board sooner with the problem. As part of the cost-cutting measures in the summer of 1986, bookmobile service replaced a staffed reading room at the East Little Rock Community Center.

Even as they took these steps, board members knew that their decisions provided only a minimal solution. Pulaski and Perry counties had not yet dealt with the shortfall caused by Amendment 59 and were operating on a 0.3 to 0.5 millage. Although there was little enthusiasm for it at the July meeting, the trustees did indeed take a proposal to restore the one-mill tax rate to the voters in the fall election. The voters of both Little Rock and Pulaski County approved the request to restore the one-mill tax rate; the voters in Perry County, however, rejected the request.

Deteriorating Building and Image

Despite these financial setbacks, the CALS board approached the city in 1987 to ask for funding to build a branch library in west Little Rock. Voters approved a bond issue that included, among other items, $1.9 million for the new branch.

Even as the board was looking at plans for a new branch, it was also looking at the state of the main library. The deterioration of the downtown area left the building in a depressed part of the city. The transient and homeless population had increased in the area, and this group used the library as a hang-out. Perceived lack of safety became a serious issue as many patrons became concerned about the problem.

The building itself left much to be desired. The 1960s architecture left little flexibility for reconfiguring the space. Makeshift "offices" had been constructed out of plywood dividers covered in carpeting. The first-floor windows were located near the ceiling, offering little natural light and adding to the gloomy atmosphere created by the general deterioration of the space. As the staff grew and technology developed, the library needed to add infrastructure such as phone lines and electrical outlets for the computers. Neither of these could be added easily because of the concrete and thick plaster used to construct the building. Bob Razer, then the head of technical services, said that to run a new line for phones or computers, "you had to use a jackhammer."

Patron and staff complaints came to the attention of the board, and the trustees grew frustrated with the administration's lack of follow-through regarding problems. The board formed a Building and Grounds Committee in late 1988 to consider improvements to the physical limitations, to deal with concerns of personal safety expressed by both patrons and employees, and to better maintain the grounds.

Trustee Tom Dillard, chair of the committee, worked with a group of Little Rock architects organized by George Wittenberg. The group met over a period of weeks to review the library building, including the way it operated, and to recommend changes.[8] This committee presented a proposal to the Board of Trustees at its June 1989 meeting that included several major changes that would update the building and make it more accessible.[9] Although the concept was well received, the revisions were not made because the board had decided to deal with a larger issue—the leadership of the library system.

A Drastic Change in Leadership

CALS trustee Sherry Walker had attended seminars on board and director evaluation at the American Library Association conference in 1988; she brought back sample evaluation forms to share with other board members. The board used these documents to assess the library, and a committee met to share the results with Martin and set goals for the year.

The process never went beyond the preliminary steps. On Wednesday, April 26, 1989, the Board of Trustees asked for Martin's resignation. Walker, board president at the time, reported that, "Over a period of time, she [Martin] has lost the confidence of the board, and she serves at the pleasure of the board...In evaluating the well-being of the system, the board felt it was time for a new director."

The board felt a growing commitment to pursue improvement and excellence in both facilities and service. To that end, they asked Bobby Roberts, then head of Archives and Special Collections at the University of Arkansas at Little Rock's Ottenheimer Library, to serve as interim director. With the change in leadership, efforts moved forward to obtain tax increases. According to Roberts, "The Board set the library on a course for quality, and they haven't looked back."

---

1 The Interlocal agreement was updated in 1977 to keep up with changes in state law. North Little Rock's Laman Library was invited to join in the agreement but declined to do so. However, in 1987, the two organizations agreed to recognize each other's library cards for borrowing privileges.

2 Heather O'Daniel, "Cataloging the Internet," *ASSOCIATES* 5 (March 1999), online at http://associates.ucr.edu/heather399.htm (accessed June 27, 2010). The legal name of the Ohio College Library Center changed to OCLC Online Computer Library Center, Inc., in 1981.

3 *Arkansas Gazette*, November 2, 1975.

4 *Arkansas Democrat*, August 1, 1979. The newspaper article about the opening of the Southwest Branch in its own building tells of a "new 1933 Dodge truck" providing service to Mabelvale, a small community just west the location of the new branch library. However, bookmobile service in Pulaski County did not start until 1938. It is likely that the bookmobile first came to the area in 1943, not 1933.

5 The children's department in the Main Library is named in honor of Ida Mae Hagin.

6 Available records do not reflect the degree to which Director Martin inspired the study, but the two-year process depended heavily on the active participation of the administration and staff. Whatever her expectations for the outcome of the study may have been, some of the findings foreshadowed questions that would be raised in later years about the effectiveness of Martin's management of the library system.

From Carnegie to Cyberspace: 100 Years at the Central Arkansas Library System

7 To remedy the situation, each affected city and county would have to pass measures to restore the full one-mill rate; state librarian Pat Murphey noted in January 1986 that only seven of the nineteen affected counties had done so. His goal, Murphey said, was that every location would restore the rate to the one-mill maximum. The State Library, which distributed state aid to local libraries, ultimately voted to cut off aid to those cities and counties that had not voted to restore their local rate. Amendment 59, which remains in place, continued to affect library funding even after the passage in 1992 of Amendment 3 that raised the cap on millage rates for libraries.

8 *Arkansas Gazette*, May 13, 1989.

9 *Arkansas Gazette*, June 3, 1989.

chapter eight

TURNING THE CORNER, 1989–1994

"The library is political. Everything in America is political."

BOBBY ROBERTS, 1998

When Bobby Roberts agreed to fill the six-month term as interim director of the Central Arkansas Library System, he took a leave of absence from his position at the University of Arkansas at Little Rock (UALR). He later applied for the permanent position, becoming the library's permanent director in October 1989. The twenty-plus years of Roberts's leadership have been a time of dramatic growth, both in the size of the library system and in the scope of its work in the community.

When Roberts arrived at CALS, he had very little experience with the system—he did not even have a CALS library card. However, his experience as a campaign aide and legislative liaison for Governor Bill Clinton and as a member of several state boards gave him insight into the political groundwork necessary to move the library system forward.

In the Interim

Rosemary Martin's sudden departure from CALS shocked Larrie Thompson, and she was uncertain what to expect when Bobby Roberts stepped in as interim director. Thompson said, "He was very easygoing. He didn't jump in and start stomping around with big boots. He very carefully sat in that back office and watched and saw how things worked. He went everyplace to know everybody… [and learned] how everything worked."

Bobby Roberts

As he evaluated the situation at CALS, Roberts found a library system that was slowly dying because of lack of funds, and also from the effects of recent years of poor management. He was impressed, however, with the quality of the staff. He found a group of talented, dedicated people who cared about the service they were giving but were working within a library system that had no sense of mission. He set about to remedy that situation by giving the staff the support they needed, putting policies into place, and dealing as quickly as possible with the funding crisis.

Roberts quickly reassured the staff that he did not see his task as the day-to-day running of the library; he trusted the skilled staff that was in place to do that. Within his first week as acting director, Roberts announced plans to create four standing staff committees: personnel, finance, automation, and collection development. He explained that he planned to focus on dealing with the politics involved—both within the system and in the community—and through that process, to find the money to develop a quality library system. His other priority centered on creating a set of policies to help guide the staff in dealing with both the public service and the behind-the-scenes running of the library. Roberts said, "The first thing I did was say, 'Let's get some policies written down about how we're going to operate.' Here's our financial policy. Here's our collection policy… A lot of those documents were around, but they weren't pulled together where there was any sort of meaningful way to look at them or add to them. You can't run an organization without policies that are approved by the board. You've got to have procedures in place."

Nevertheless, two issues that had to do with the daily operations were high on Roberts's list of priorities: improving the appearance and the maintenance of the library facilities and dealing with security issues. Suggestions in response to a 1986 marketing study on improving the public library included "separate readers from loiterers," and "stop bums from hanging around." Many parents hesitated to bring their children to activities at the downtown location because of the number of vagrants in the area. Whereas Rosemary Martin had not dealt aggressively with such security issues, Roberts had no trouble establishing rules for those who spent time at the library and enforcing those rules.

Several staff members related an example that contrasted Martin's and Roberts's management styles. When Martin was director, an unstable patron began verbally abusing the circulation staff and quickly became agitated. Martin quietly locked the door in the decorative grate that separated the administration area from the public service area, returned to her office, and left the staff to deal with the patron. Not long after Roberts became director, a similar incident occurred. Roberts heard the commotion and came running out of the administration area to deal with the patron. He told the man that he could leave the library on his own or wait until the police arrived and be escorted out.

For the staff, this story exemplified a major change taking place at the library: Whereas Martin tended to run away from problems, Roberts ran toward them. A 1990 issue of *The Journal of Library Administration* featured an article titled "Public Librarians as Employers: Expectations," written by Martin. One paragraph seems to particularly reflect her mindset during her time at CALS: "We are taught that a public library's doors are open to all. Does that 'all' include the many homeless people with less-than-ideal personal hygiene who fill up reading rooms, create disturbances, and make the more ordinary citizen afraid to enter? Where do we acquire the skills to quickly evaluate a potentially dangerous situation and to immediately act rather than stand helplessly by while the situation gets out of control? What happened to the quiet, intellectual environment that was described in library education?"

Melinda Jackson was introduced to Roberts's hands-on style one rainy night about a month after his arrival. The flat roof at the Fletcher Branch cracked, leaving about a fifteen-foot break. Jackson said, "It was raining heavily—right over our mystery collection. I called Main looking desperately for anybody I could find. I got Bobby, who happened to be in his office. He came out there. Not only did he get it fixed, he went up and helped tar the roof. I knew it was a new era right there."

Roberts not only was more visible to the staff, but also was more visible in the community than Martin. Linda Bly said, "He put a face to the library that had not been there for a long time."

BOBBY ROBERTS'S FIRST MESSAGE TO THE STAFF

The May 1989 issue of *The Network*, the CALS staff newsletter, included a message from Bobby Roberts that read:

"For the past few days you may have encountered someone wandering through your library who appeared to be slightly lost but interested in what he saw. The person with the curious look on his face was probably me, your new interim director. Moving from academics to public library service in one week was a big leap for me, and I am certain that it was a surprise for you.

"During the next few weeks I will be learning about our overall operation and I will also be meeting all of the members of the staff. I have much to learn from you and I hope that you will be patient with me as I learn more about our system. Like any student I am curious so please pardon me if I seem to be full of questions about how you perform your various duties. I am sure that you are all good teachers and I am always eager to learn.

"I am honored to have been asked by the board to serve as your interim director. I think that it will be an opportunity for me to apply skills that I have acquired in both academic libraries and government service in a new setting. I hope that it will also be a rewarding experience for you."

West Little Rock Branch Opens

The unnamed west Little Rock branch was under construction when Bobby Roberts took over as interim director of CALS in May 1989. By the time the branch opened in April 1990 as the Adolphine Fletcher Terry Library, Roberts had been selected as Rosemary Martin's replacement as director.

The Terry Branch marked a turning point for the library for several reasons. The Terry Branch made library service available in the fastest-growing area of Little Rock. It also was the first new branch construction completely under the control of CALS; other branches had been inherited as part of the merger with the Pulaski–Perry system or had been completed by city governments on behalf of the library.

The CALS Board of Trustees actively participated in the planning for the new branch and had a definite vision for what they wanted the branch to be. They wanted to invest in the branch as an architecturally significant, public building that would be a point of pride for the community it served.

Opening-day statistics for the Terry Branch broke all previous records for CALS. An estimated crowd of 5,500 checked out 3,185 books—approximately 6.6 books per minute. Previously, the circulation record had been 1,943 at the Fletcher Library. Average daily circulation for the entire system, before the addition of the Terry Branch, was approximately 2,600. The staff issued 443 new library cards on the first day, which far exceeded the system's average of 78 cards per day.

The Terry branch also served as the catalyst for launching CALS's art program. Prior to this time, CALS owned a few pieces of art that had been donated by patrons over the years but was not in the business of collecting art. Using money from the Morris Fund, the library commissioned a colorful cloth appliqué from Nancy Jo Collins, a well-known folk artist from Floral (Independence County). The piece, which depicts a rural, one-room library with children playing in front of the building, was intended to hang in the children's area of the Terry Branch. However, the staff could not find a suitable place to hang the work, so it was moved to the Youth Services Department of the Main Library.

In the September 1990 issue of *The Network*, Bob Razer explained the art program by saying, "Priority will be given to Arkansas artists in any purchase, though all types of art are eligible for potential purchase. After a few years, we hope CALS will have several types of artwork and a diversity of styles with many different Arkansas artists represented in our collection. This aspect of the Morris Fund will not only add to employees' working environment, but will add to library users' visits to our libraries as well."

Improving Morale

The coming of Bobby Roberts and the opening of the Terry Branch boosted staff morale. In Roberts, staff members saw a leader who appreciated their skills and who was willing to work hard to solve the problems facing the library. In the Terry Branch, they saw a glimpse of the library as it could be—buildings that served as architectural sources of pride for the community instead of utilitarian boxes to hold books.

Roberts promoted two known quantities to assistant director positions: Linda Bly handled everything on the public service side of the library, and Bob Razer the technical services side.

This new structure accomplished two things. It made two people who had significant experience with CALS responsible for the workings of the library, and it freed Roberts to work with the Board of Trustees to put policies and procedures in place as well as to build relationships in the community that would help to solve the funding problems that plagued the library.

The library's budget did not give Roberts much to work with for improving staff salaries, but he implemented other creative ways to improve working conditions for the staff—such as using Morris Fund money to purchase art. He also spearheaded an effort to make zero-interest, short-term loans available to staff members for financial emergencies. The Boodle Fund was established in 1990 and relied on money earned from recycling aluminum cans and newspapers. The fund started with a balance of $350 and has grown to more than $9,000.

Although the staff responded well to Roberts's support, enthusiasm, and creativity, they remained hampered by budget constraints. For several years, the staff had to stop purchasing new books during the second half of each year because the money ran out. This practice was devastating to the collection because the staff could never catch up with the backlog of items published after purchasing ceased each year.

Developing the Youth Services Program

The children's department was hit particularly hard by the budget constraints because the book budget for juvenile materials often was cut to nothing as the library tried to keep up with the demand for current best-sellers in the adult section.

When Bettye Kerns joined CALS in 1990, children's programming consisted of weekly story time programs for the three-to-five age group and the summer reading program for older children. Kerns says that she relied on the FOCAL group to provide funds for the materials needed for the summer reading club because the library's budget could not support the youth programs.

Bobby Roberts hired Kerns to expand the library's services to children and to build relationships with the schools to make better use of the library. Kerns pushed to train the youth programmers at the branches in ways to make the children's programming more attractive. She says that youth programming was being done the same way it had been done forever—mostly a librarian standing up in front of a group of children reading from a picture book.

Competition from television and other forms of readily available entertainment meant that the library had to develop more creative programming—on a shoestring budget. Kerns wanted to include programming for all age groups, so she reached out to the community to bring in speakers from a wide variety of sources—zookeepers brought in animals, hobbyists talked about their special interests—and attendance began to grow significantly. In 1990, the library provided 609 programs; by the end of 2009, that number had grown to 3,722.

BOODLE FUND

Bob Razer explained the origins of the name for the Boodle Fund in the staff newsletter: "One of the major events of late 19th and early 20th century urban American history was the role played by the Tammany Hall organization in New York City politics. A leader of that colorful group was George Washington Plunkitt, ward boss for one of the city's Assembly districts. Plunkitt made no bones about what his organization did and why it was worthwhile.

Anyone receiving a city contract, license or franchise was expected to provide a kickback or payoff to city officials. Bribes also were welcomed. All this was acceptable revenue, in Plunkitt's view, and was considered 'honest graft' or 'boodle' as opposed to 'black graft' such as vice or extortion. Plunkitt considered boodle as just reward for public service, an occupation that was normally underpaid. The more successful your organization, the more boodle you received."

SKY THE SEA MONSTER

In 1991, the children's department unveiled a twelve-foot-long sea monster carved out of plastic foam. Its belly contained eight feet of shelf space for children's books. Designed by library employees Michael Chambers and Cherece Watson, the creature was painted electric blue with green speckles. The scales on its back were made from iridescent polyester film. Jacqueline Groce, then a 4th grader at the Cathedral School, suggested the name Sky because of the monster's beautiful blue color and curved design. Other names considered were "Bookasaurus," "Bluey," and "Loch Ness Jr."

Kerns also had strong beliefs about collection development, reflecting a personal experience she had in 1972 when she was practice-teaching. Her class had read a book about a rabbit who wanted wings so he could fly like a bird. She had the class talk about things they wished they could change about themselves. Most of the children had predictable answers—girls with curly hair wanted straight hair and vice versa. But, one boy responded by saying, "I'd be white."

Kerns said, "It floored me—absolutely floored me. His self image was that he was nothing if he wasn't white." She was especially shocked because this child was one of the most popular children in the class. When she became a children's librarian, she deliberately sought out diverse books with "African-American people, and Asian-American people, and gay people, and whatever kind of people" that were depicted in normal lives. She said she wanted to expose kids to those books so "they could go in and find themselves in that book and find a person that they wanted to be."

She also strongly believes that the public library has a responsibility to include books that depict children in all kinds of family settings—two parents, one parent, same-sex parents, etc. She said, "Children need to be able come into our library and find a picture book that is reflective of their parents, of their family—that reflects it as normal. This isn't about religion or if it is right, wrong, or whatever. To me, it's not about an issue. It's about children. Every child has the right to find themselves in a book and say 'that was me.'"

Bettye Kerns working in the Rarin'-to-Read Mobile children's bookmobile.
Photo courtesy of Bettye Kerns

Changing the Constitution

Roberts's initial efforts to give the library a better public image, improve working conditions for the staff, and proactively address the problems of the system won him the support of the staff. He already had the strong support and confidence of the Board of Trustees. In fact, he inherited a board that had made a deliberate decision to grow the library from an adequate system to an excellent system. The board also consciously decided that, as the library was able to expand, new facilities would reflect this commitment. The board was determined to use the growth and building process itself as a way to help foster community identity. Roberts said, "We really try to build these [buildings] where people will go in and go, 'Wow! We're glad we spent the money on this.'"

In order to deal with the ongoing funding issues, Roberts and the board first had to focus on getting a constitutional amendment to lift the fifty-year-old one-mill cap on library taxes. This required two efforts: first to get the needed amendments on the ballot and then to generate statewide voter support for the general election. Because CALS was the largest library system in the state, Roberts knew it would have to provide the leadership for the movement.

The library launched a major publicity campaign to support passage of Amendment 3.

Still, the effort had to be statewide and involve library supporters from around the state, as well as the Arkansas Library Association. CALS Board of Trustees president Sherry Walker, an experienced legislative lobbyist, was also executive director of the Arkansas Library Association and had led it and other library organizations in the successful 1989 effort to get the law passed ensuring confidentiality of patron records. This brought public libraries to the attention of the people and produced a favorable political climate for dealing with the funding issue. Walker served as political consultant for the nearly two-year-long library tax amendment campaign, an effort that lasted from the 1991 legislative session through the 1992 general election.

Amendments can get on the ballot in Arkansas either through the petition process or through a decision of the legislature. Because the petition process had been tried earlier for the library tax question and failed, and because of Roberts's extensive political connections, the organizers decided to go through the legislature for this effort.[1]

Roberts put his political savvy and connections to work to move the library tax amendment forward. When Governor Clinton approached him about working for him during the 1991 session, the Board of Trustees agreed to give Roberts the leave of absence he needed if Clinton would agree to support the constitutional amendment on library taxes.

The proposed amendment would raise the cap both for cities of more than 5,000 and also for counties from one mill to five mills for library operations.[2] Recognizing that even five mills could quickly become inadequate, leaders included a provision that allowed voters to approve an additional three mills for capital improvement for libraries, again for both cities and counties.

Fritz DeBrine, Jennifer Chilcoat, and Verna Lacy tough out the soaring temperatures while the building was without air conditioning.

Photo courtesy of Jennifer Chilcoat

THE SUMMER OF '92

The political scene was not the only thing to heat up during the summer of 1992. When CALS staff came back from the 4th of July holiday, they discovered that the ancient air-conditioning system had died. The system was so old that it had to be sent to Atlanta for repair and Freon replacement, so the Main Library had no air conditioning for approximately six weeks.

Staff who sweltered through those six weeks remember the sherbet and Gatorade the administration kept stocked in the staff lounge, getting to wear shorts to work, and security guard Vernon Johnson—who wore short sleeves in the dead of winter—patrolling the building wrapped in a wet towel and carrying a hand-held fan.

The effort to put the library amendment on the ballot succeeded, and supporters turned their attention to the election, which would take place in November 1992.

The board decided to modify its planned activities for 1992 so staff could concentrate on getting the amendment passed.[3] Most importantly, the State Library decided to use federal grant money available to the state through the Library Services and Construction Act for a public relations campaign on library use in general. This campaign, which could not legally be used to solicit votes, kept the public library in the minds of the people during the long time period between when the legislature put the amendment on the ballot and when it would come before the voters.

In addition to these public relations efforts, a strong campaign that was funded by private donations of approximately $130,000 focused directly on persuading the voters to approve the amendment. All of these efforts paid off. The library tax amendment, which was on the same ballot as Bill Clinton's bid for the presidency, was carried by a larger percentage of the population than voted for Clinton. Bob Razer joked that "Clinton rode the library amendment coattails to the White House."[4]

---

1 The legislature is allowed to put three amendments on the ballot every two years; since many amendments may be proposed, narrowing it down to three can be a challenge. According to custom, each house gets to choose one amendment, and they then jointly agree on the third amendment. Although a wide variety of amendments were proposed, when asked, Clinton always gave the library amendment first place. Passage was certain if it came to the floor; the challenge was to get it reported out of committee in both the Senate and the House. Supporters realized they needed to work within the perceived rural-urban split in the legislature and demonstrate sponsorship from around the state and not just in Little Rock. The principal tool used for ensuring passage of the amendment was being sure that legislators received a lot of phone calls when they were going to vote for a library issue.

2 The five-mill cap was chosen because this is the same limit imposed on cities and counties for their operations.

3 Bob Razer, "The Library, YES! The 1992 Amendment 3 Campaign," *Arkansas Libraries* 50 (April 1993): 5–14.

4 The library amendment carried with 59 percent of the vote; Clinton received 53 percent of the vote in Arkansas.

chapter nine

CALS COMES OF AGE, 1994–2010

"It's funny that we think of libraries as quiet demure places where we are shushed by dusty, bun-balancing, bespectacled women. The truth is libraries are raucous clubhouses for free speech, controversy and community. Librarians have stood up to the Patriot Act, sat down with noisy toddlers and reached out to illiterate adults. Libraries can never be shushed."

PAULA POUNDSTONE, COMEDIAN AND AUTHOR

After the constitutional amendment passed in 1992, Roberts turned his attention to the specific elections that needed to be held in the various areas CALS served. The public responded enthusiastically.

In 1993, CALS won four elections at one time to support the library system. Little Rock voters approved an $18 million bond issue providing for a new building for the Fletcher Library, a midtown branch, and relocation of the Main Library, along with funding for the automation of the entire library system. The Little Rock voters also approved one mill for operations. County voters approved an increase of 0.6 mill for library operational and maintenance costs. In the same election, Maumelle voters approved a $1 million bond to build its library.

Since 1993, CALS has issued approximately $93 million of bonds for capital improvements. All but $4.7 million of the bonds have been municipal bonds that are approved by the public with a millage to repay them. The branch buildings that have been constructed are legally owned by the cities but are dedicated to library use. [1]

With funding in place, CALS entered into the era of branch construction, most of which has been under the direction of Linda Bly.

Little Rock took the library out of its city budget in 1993, after the millage cap was lifted and the additional millages were approved. Today, 90 to 93 percent of the system's primary income is generated from property taxes in four different political jurisdictions. A small portion comes from the state through the State Library; the balance of the income comes from interest, fees, and other miscellaneous income. The library's highly complex finances are a far cry from the days when the treasurer of the Board of Trustees wrote and signed all of the checks for the library during the monthly board meeting.

Increased funding, automation of the library, advances in technology, and the Board of Trustees' commitment to expansion and to providing quality buildings jump-started CALS's most dramatic period of expansion.

Automation

In March 1994, CALS announced the beginning of a major project to bring automation to the library system through technology. When Bob Razer announced the automation project, he explained that the library would have an online catalog and an automated circulation system. He added that CALS would have state-of-the-art technology for acquisitions, serials, reference, and collection management needs and concluded by saying, "Also we will have provided library users with access to the emerging information highway we read so much about."[2]

Razer assembled a staff committee to manage the project with charter members Bobby Roberts, Linda Bly, Melinda Jackson, and Bob Razer from administration; Peggy Machen and Wayne Morrow from circulation; Phillip Jones and Fritz DeBrine from reference; Tracy Hamby and Tim Nutt from cataloging; Valerie Thwing from interlibrary loan; and Diane Hudson from the Nixon Branch. Including representatives from all the stakeholder departments allowed the committee to consider all aspects of the project and ensured that the needs of all areas would be met.

The process included choosing a software system, purchasing and installing the computer hardware, and training the staff. After the initial decisions were made and the hardware was in place, every book already in the system had to be relabeled with a barcode to allow for electronic processing of acquisition and circulation. Each branch had to be closed briefly while crews of staff members moved in to re-label the books and remove the card catalogs. The entire process took more than three years to complete.

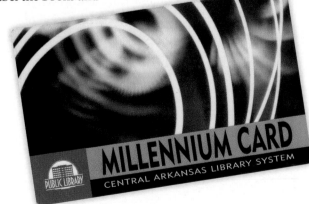

Automation also allowed CALS to issue new, scanable patron cards. The Millennium CALS card replaced the original scanable card—a new design for a new millennium.

From Carnegie to Cyberspace: 100 Years at the Central Arkansas Library System

Gateway Card

In 1995, CALS expanded the library's reach as well as the reach of its patrons by championing the Gateway Card system, which allowed residents in Arkansas, Cleveland, Conway, Dallas, Faulkner, Garland, Grant, Hot Spring, Jackson, Jefferson, Lonoke, Montgomery, Perry, Polk, Pope, Prairie, Pulaski, Saline, Van Buren, and White counties to check out books from any participating library without having to pay a non-resident fee.

Prior to this agreement, CALS charged a non-resident fee of approximately sixty dollars per year to everyone who used the library services but did not live within the library's service area (because those patrons did not support the operational costs of the library through their tax dollars).

Melinda Jackson worked with librarians at the other area libraries. They received a Library Services and Construction Act grant to test the program for a year. The program was a success; Jackson says it remains popular because so many people commute and need to access a library near where they work.

Roberts's expansive view toward library service was summed up when he said, "We ought to make information freely and easily accessible all through Central Arkansas. We all have a vested interest in people getting smarter; we don't have any interest in everybody getting dumber...We should do everything we can to encourage [sharing information]. We shouldn't put up any barriers in the way of people getting information."

A New Main Library

The board had discussed the need for expansion of the Main Library facility a decade earlier, but lack of funding and lack of agreement on how to proceed had prevented it from taking action. After the 1993 bond issue passed, Roberts and the board began discussing options for moving the library. The existing location presented too many problems—no space for expansion, poor parking options, security issues—so the board started considering other locations.

The Board of Trustees considered relocating the Main Library to a relatively undeveloped midtown area, but they concluded that it should remain downtown. They considered both the empty *Arkansas Gazette* building at 3rd and Louisiana streets and the old Federal Reserve building located across the street from the *Gazette* building, but neither had the load-bearing capacity needed for a library. They also looked at the old Terminal Warehouse building located at 500 East Markham Street, but it was too large and too expensive.

The Fones Building came to Roberts's attention through his friend Bill Spivey. The building was in bankruptcy, and Spivey thought it would be a good location for the library. Roberts had no particular interest in the building, but he agreed to look at it.

The building, which was constructed in 1920 as the warehouse for Fones Bros. Hardware, had several advantages that appealed to Roberts, Bly, and the architects. Its concrete floors and columns had the load-bearing capacity the library needed to support the weight of the shelves and thousands of books; it was located next to Interstate 30 and the Markham Street exit, which made it

HEAVY LOAD

Load-bearing capacity for a library building is significantly higher than for most buildings—approximately 250 pounds per foot as compared to 75 pounds per foot for an office building—because of the extraordinary weight of the books and shelving.

easily accessible and highly visible; and the foreclosure status made the price easily within the library's budget.

Restoring an old building appealed to the historian in Roberts, and making a commitment to revitalizing the river-front area—then largely a deteriorating warehouse district—appealed to his vision of the library as an agent of change.

During the planning and construction of the new facility, Roberts's vision of how the library could contribute to the revitalization of the area was challenged by myriad details. "When we started construction," Roberts said, "there were five inches of water in the basement and two inches of pigeon droppings upstairs." Although the building budget accounted for cleaning up hazardous material such as asbestos and lead paint, the pigeon droppings were a costly surprise that added more than $125,000 to the cleanup costs.

The Fones Building consisted of five floors and a basement, for a total of 156,000 square feet. It provided substantially more floor space than the old location in just the first three floors alone. Initially, the top floor was left unfinished, and the fourth floor, while finished, was not fully occupied.

The library building on Louisiana Street closed in July 1997 to allow time for preparations for the move. Jennifer Chilcoat had developed a system for moving the books and other materials when she oversaw the move of the Fletcher Branch from its original location to its current location in 1996. Instead of moving books shelf by shelf to keep everything in Dewey Decimal order, Chilcoat pre-planned the move by mapping out the new location of every shelf of books and developing a tagging system to let the people doing the move know where each shelf of books was moving to.

One team moved books from the old shelves to large carts. The first book of each section had a green bookmark with a shelf number and the last book of each shelf had a red bookmark with the same number. The corresponding shelf in the new building was tagged with this number. Chilcoat's system sped up the moving process because multiple teams could work in different areas of the shelves to load books, and all the reshelving teams needed to do was find the correct shelf number when unloading the books.

The Fones Building before renovation.

The renovated Fones Building as the new Main Library.

From Carnegie to Cyberspace: 100 Years at the Central Arkansas Library System

Chilcoat used the same system for the Main Library move. Whereas the Fletcher move involved rolling the carts across a parking lot to the new building, the Main move involved loading the carts onto large trucks and transporting them to the new location. The move to Main took only three days using Chilcoat's system.

After all of the materials were moved and arranged, the staff focused on making final adjustments to get the new building ready, and the new Main Library opened on September 20, 1997.

Librarian of the Year

In six years, Bobby Roberts had transformed CALS from a system struggling to survive to a system poised for explosive growth and development. Passage of the constitutional amendment that allowed for increased millage set the stage not only for CALS's growth, but also aided library development across the state.

Library Journal named Roberts its 1997 Librarian of the Year. Many of the staff members traveled to New Orleans for the award presentation banquet. At one point, the emcee asked all of the CALS staff present to stand for recognition and asked each one to say something about Roberts. Linda Bly responded by saying that the three most frightening words you can hear come out of Bobby Roberts's mouth are "I've been thinking."

Many staff members have used that anecdote in the ensuing years, but Jennifer Chilcoat added that equally frightening are the words, "I don't see any reason why we can't…"

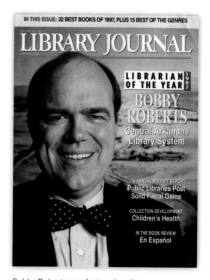

Bobby Roberts was featured on the cover of *Library Journal* when he was named 1997 Librarian of the Year.

Growth and Development

In its first year of operation, the new Main Library experienced a 50 percent increase in circulation. Roberts, who first thought the greatest potential for the new location would be to serve the downtown business community, was surprised at the extent to which family and children's programming and circulation increased. In addition, the location and the improved facility proved attractive to organizations in need of public meeting space. The old library hosted fifteen to twenty meetings a month; in June 1998, the facility hosted 120 meetings.

The public relations department launched an ad campaign to promote the new library. Each ad prominently featured the new logo for the library system, which included a silhouette of the new Main Library and the phrase "public library" instead of "Central Arkansas Library System." Roberts wanted to reinforce, at every opportunity, the public's connection with the library system to help foster community pride and a sense of ownership.

The new building provided ample space to expand the library's collection and services, and Roberts worked to raise funds to support this growth. For example, the demand for local history and genealogy materials continued to grow, and Roberts worked with FOCAL to launch the Historic Arkansas Project in 1996, which focused on increasing the collection of historical material and on disseminating that history to the people.

top: Ads promoting the new Main Library featured literary quotes paired with clever promotional information. This ad, featuring a quote from Francis Bacon, also lets patrons know that the Main Library had 1,300 cookbooks as well as ten books on indigestion.

bottom: The library's campaign to reach out to the growing Spanish-speaking community included this ad inviting them to escape the heat by visiting the library.

The Butler Center for Arkansas Studies, created in 1997 through an endowment by Richard C. Butler Sr., incorporated the existing Arkansas history and genealogy collection along with the materials purchased through the Historic Arkansas Project into an archive and research center. The center's mission focused on promoting a greater understanding and appreciation of Arkansas history, literature, art, and culture. Tom Dillard, a historian and long-time promoter of Arkansas history who had served on the library's Board of Trustees, joined the library staff as curator of the Butler Center.

The library also made a commitment to increasing community access to electronic information. Surveys conducted among patrons as early as 1982 showed that patrons were already calling for more computer access in the libraries. In 1999, CALS received 34 computers as part of the Gates Library Initiative, administered in Arkansas by the Arkansas State Library. The Gates Foundation grants also helped fund training for staff members, as well as providing software from Microsoft.[3]

Funding from the Roy and Christine Sturgis Foundation allowed the library to create the Sturgis Computer Lab on the fourth floor of the new building, which provided public access to computers as well as a venue to offer training to library staff and computer technology classes for the public.[4]

The increased space at the Main Library coupled with more operational funding and endowments allowed for the expansion of adult programming—including establishing a distinguished lecture series with three endowed lectures per year: the Ira Sanders Distinguished Lecture, the Fred Darragh Distinguished Lecture, and the J. N. Heiskell Distinguished Lecture. Fred Darragh, a former CALS board member and longtime library supporter, provided a gift to endow the lecture series.

Roberts's enthusiasm inspired other managers at the library to explore new opportunities. According to census data, the Hispanic population in Pulaski County had grown by 41 percent from 1990 to 1999. In December 2001, CALS announced that it would have books in Spanish available at three locations—the Main Library, the Sanders Branch in Sherwood, and the Southwest Branch. The Spanish collection consisted of approximately 200 books purchased through bond money as well as through a grant funded by the Chamberlin family and the June Hoes Williams family through the Arkansas Community Foundation. Almeta Smith, branch librarian at Southwest, had applied for the grant support for a project titled "Exploradores de Libros," a literacy project she developed for the children of Hispanic immigrants who used the Southwest Library.

Revising the Interlocal Agreement

Because the library system involves multiple local governments, it is governed by an Interlocal Agreement. On November 17, 1998, a new Interlocal Agreement was approved that replaced the 1977 document. Among other things, the new agreement gave the library system the right to buy and sell land, to acquire land through eminent domain, and to receive bond revenues. These changes affected planning for new library branches, as well as the way property is administered and maintained. Essentially, it allowed CALS to have more control over the buildings and to be less dependent on local political jurisdictions for improvements and maintenance.[5]

The new agreement also increased the number of board members from nine to thirteen and specified that each jurisdiction in which the system operated would be represented. The new configuration consisted of:

- seven representatives from Little Rock (appointed by the Little Rock City Board of Directors)

- two representatives from Pulaski County, exclusive of North Little Rock (appointed by the Pulaski County Judge, with approval of the Pulaski County Court)

- one representative from Perry County (appointed by the Perry County Quorum Court)

- one representative from Sherwood (appointed by the Sherwood City Council)

- one representative from Jacksonville (appointed by the Jacksonville City Council)

- one representative from Maumelle (appointed by the City of Maumelle Board of Directors)

New Challenges to Patron Privacy

The Uniting and Strengthening America by Providing Appropriate Tools Required to Intercept and Obstruct Terrorism (USA PATRIOT) Act, enacted after the terrorist attacks of September 11, 2001, was not the first challenge to libraries' commitment to the privacy of patrons' records, but this act marked the first time in recent history when the assumption of privacy was seriously challenged.

Questions of confidentiality and intellectual freedom have come up several times in the library's history. The Arkansas Library Association published a manual for librarians to use in dealing with questions of intellectual freedom. The manual, designed by the Arkansas Library Association's Intellectual Freedom Committee and modeled on a similar manual published by the American Library Association, was first published in 1982, and it was revised in 1987 and 1993.[6] In 1989, the Arkansas State Legislature passed Act 903, which removed library records from the Freedom of Information Act and thus ensured the confidentiality of patron records.

The USA PATRIOT Act gave specific legal status to what thirty years earlier was initially justified as merely an investigative technique. A previous act, the 1978 Foreign Intelligence Security Act, had set specific limitations on the federal government's right to investigate and accumulate information on individuals without probable cause. Investigators had to obtain a so-called FISA warrant to justify requiring organizations such as libraries and hospitals to produce otherwise private information about individuals, with evidence that those being investigated presented a clear threat. Section 215 of the PATRIOT Act sharply reduced the level of proof required and broadened the scope of what information could be gathered.

In the years since the confidentiality issue was first raised, libraries have become the major public access point for Internet use, in addition to libraries automating their own record keeping. While the technology provides more information of potential interest to investigators, it also provides the means to protect patrons' records. Because of the commitment to patron privacy, library computers were programmed to dump circulation records at the end of the day. This is also done with website cache information on computer terminals.

When the impact of the act was discussed, Roberts informed staff that if they were presented with the appropriate court order, they would have to provide the information being requested. Nevertheless, he remained confident that patron privacy could still be protected. "I think because of the automated systems," Roberts said, "[potential investigators] aren't going to get much."

Bobby Roberts takes the stage at the grand opening of the Arkansas Studies Institute with former governors Dale Bumpers, David Pryor, Jim Guy Tucker, and current governor Mike Beebe looking on.

From Carnegie to Cyberspace: 100 Years at the Central Arkansas Library System

"I've Been Thinking"

Roberts initiated a series of innovative projects that pushed the envelope of traditional library service. Roberts says that many of these ideas came together from a lot of smaller ideas and random thoughts. Perhaps the best example of this confluence of ideas stands at the corner of President Clinton Avenue and Rock Street—the Arkansas Studies Institute (ASI).

The ASI is a joint project of CALS and the University of Arkansas at Little Rock (UALR) that combines the holdings of the Butler Center for Arkansas Studies and UALR's Archives and Special Collections. The institute's combined collection includes the gubernatorial papers of six Arkansas governors: Carl Bailey, Winthrop Rockefeller, Dale Bumpers, Frank White, Bill Clinton, and Jim Guy Tucker.

The idea for the institute grew out of a series of unrelated events:

- In 1978, Roberts started the special collections program at UALR. But he also knew that the UALR library's resources were focused in other, more pressing areas

- In 1992, Arkansans voted to create term limits for the Arkansas legislature—which meant that, in 1998, approximately half of the existing legislative seats were filled by newcomers. Roberts toyed with the idea of creating a legislative boot camp to help acclimate the new legislators to the state's political history.

- In 1997, Bill Clinton selected Little Rock as the home for the Clinton Presidential Library. Roberts put together a proposal for CALS to house his gubernatorial papers.

Each of these things stayed in Roberts's head and meshed with other ideas he had for developing the downtown library campus as well as with his personal interest in history.

The concept of making it easier for the public to connect with Arkansas history, politics, and culture lay at the core of all of these thoughts. Roberts struck a deal with Joel Anderson, chancellor of UALR, and on June 25, 2003, they announced the plan to create the Alliance for the Study of Arkansas History and Politics. Former president Bill Clinton spoke at the press conference, saying, "I want all these records together because I want people to know more about Arkansas history…I want them to see how in these various governors' terms the states really were laboratories of democracy in many ways."

Six years later, the Arkansas Studies Institute (the new name for the project) opened. UALR chancellor Joel Anderson said, "I know many of the historians and political scientists in Arkansas personally, and I think many of them would say that too little scholarly work has been done on our state's history and government due to a lack of available and accessible primary materials. This new partnership will bring into one building a critical mass of available and accessible primary materials."

ENCYCLOPEDIA OF ARKANSAS

When the staff of the Encyclopedia of Arkansas History & Culture (EOA) wrote their first grant applications, they estimated that the encyclopedia would receive 50,000 hits per month. During the first half of 2010, the EOA website averaged more than 3,000,000 hits per month from visitors in 187 countries. CALS is the only library system in the nation to host a state encyclopedia.

As Roberts's idea continued to grow, it included more partners and more real estate. The final plan consisted of restoring two existing buildings (the Porbeck & Bowman building and the Geyer & Adams building) and combining them with a new, all-glass building that could hold the weight of the archival collections. The conglomerate building ended up housing the UALR and Butler Center holdings, Butler Center offices, offices for the UALR archival staff, the UA Clinton School of Public Service's downtown campus, four art galleries, a series of meeting rooms that UALR also uses as classrooms for some of its graduate classes, the Arkansas Humanities Council offices, and the business offices of *The Oxford American* magazine. Part of the first-floor space is earmarked to become the Concordia Hall Museum in the near future.

Roberts said, "It just seemed to me that it makes sense to partner up with as many people as you can who are doing the same thing that you are. That if you can do it, and do it in a way that everybody benefits from it, you're better off."

Even as all of the pieces were coming together for the ASI, Roberts was thinking about other projects to expand the library.

In 2001, the library opened the Cox Creative Center on the Main Library campus. This renovated building houses the library's "gently read" used bookstore, gift shop, and café. Roberts wanted to move beyond the traditional library book sale to create a year-round opportunity for the public to purchase books.

A co-op of Arkansas artists approached Roberts about using part of the space in the Cox Center as a gallery for Arkansas artists. Roberts thought the partnership was a good idea because it would create a venue to showcase some of the library's art and would help Arkansas artists promote their work. The library eventually took over running the art gallery, which remained in the Cox Center until it moved to the Arkansas Studies Institute in 2009.

Roberts's philosophy of partnering with like-minded people came into play again in 2005 when the library became a partner in the 2nd Friday Art Night program—a monthly evening of art sponsored by downtown galleries and museums. The inaugural participants on March 11, 2005, were Amy Howard Richmond Fine Art, River Market ArtSpace, AfrJaMex, Hearne Fine Art, Clinton Museum Store, CALS, Oval Art Gallery, and the Historic Arkansas Museum.

Roberts and Tom Dillard had long discussed the need for a comprehensive and reliable reference work on Arkansas—especially for the educators who were required to teach Arkansas history but lacked the resources to do it effectively. Roberts approved a plan to create an online encyclopedia for the state and, in 2002, Dillard began planning an extensive project to create the online Encyclopedia of Arkansas History & Culture (EOA). Tim Nutt initially served as managing editor and Jill Curran as the project coordinator. The project received a $1.2 million grant from the Winthrop Rockefeller Foundation and additional funding from the Department of Arkansas Heritage, Arkansas Humanities Council, other grants, and individual donations.

Dillard left the Butler Center in 2004; Nutt and Curran left in 2005. David Stricklin, who replaced Dillard as head of the Butler Center, promoted Nathania Sawyer from senior editor for the encyclopedia to project manager, and the online encyclopedia launched as a work in progress in May 2006. Many other states have created encyclopedias through humanities councils, universities, and other organizations, but the EOA is the only state encyclopedia created by a public library system.

In 2007, CALS became home to a three-year Shoah Foundation[7] initiative that incorporates a series of video testimonials from Holocaust survivors and other witnesses as a teaching tool for the classroom. The initial collection consisted of 24 videos, including four that were filmed in Arkansas. The Testimony to Tolerance Initiative provided DVD copies of the videos for the CALS collection as well as providing funding for an initiative coordinator at CALS who would conduct workshops for middle school and high school educators.[8]

Participants at the Arkansas Literary Festival have the opportunity to meet authors and purchase signed copies of those authors' books.

Another extraordinary opportunity came when CALS took over management of the Arkansas Literary Festival in July 2008. The festival began in 2004 as a project of the Arkansas Literary Councils Inc., with the proceeds going to nonprofit adult literacy programs throughout the state. Speakers include both nationally recognized and emerging writers who read from and talk about their books. Many of the featured authors are native Arkansans or have a connection to the state. In 2010, more than sixty authors participated in the festival.

CALS Looks Ahead

Bobby Roberts transformed CALS from a moderately successful, relatively small library system into a spectacularly successful one. The key ingredients in this growth have been his vision, political insight and skills, and understanding of methods of finance—paired with a strong staff and a forward-looking Board of Trustees.

According to David Stricklin, "[Roberts] has the uncommon quality of being able to juggle the big picture and lots of little pictures. He knows a great deal about public finance and has the administrative and political skills to get things done. He has used these skills not only to get money for the system, but also to organize and use it effectively and without any hint of impropriety."

As much as Roberts likes to think creatively, he never forgets the core mission of the library. During his twenty-plus years as director, older branches have been updated, five new branches have been added to the system and, as of 2010, two more are under construction or are on the drawing board. These branches are much more than extensions of the Main Library. They are CALS's way of meeting its public where they live and providing the unique collection of materials and services that make the branches vital partners in the communities they serve.

1 Today, the only exceptions are the branches in Maumelle and Perry County, which are owned by CALS.

2 Bob Razer, "Automation Bits & Bytes," *The Network* (March 1994).

3 The Gates Library Foundation was established in 1997 by Bill and Melinda Gates in the belief that public libraries could "play an important role in helping bridge the looming digital divide, and bring computers and the Internet to everyone." They focused first on bringing access to the Internet to underserved areas, based on U.S. Census Bureau poverty statistics. Following the initial efforts in Louisiana and Alabama, Arkansas, New Mexico, Kentucky, West Virginia and Mississippi were chosen in 1998 to receive statewide partnership grants. *98 Annual Reports for the William H. Gates Foundation and the Gates Library Foundation*, available online at http://www.gatesfoundation.org (accessed July 14, 2010).

4 Eventually, public-use computer terminals were installed in all the branch libraries, and, in 2009, laptops became available to be checked out and used in the libraries.

5 Although library buildings, with the exception of the Sanders Library in Sherwood, technically belong to the cities where they are located, they can be used only as libraries. CALS has responsibility for maintenance and repairs.

6 Ethel Ambrose of CALS served on the initial Intellectual Freedom Committee, and Bettye Kerns currently serves on the committee.

7 The Shoah Foundation was established in 1994 by Steven Spielberg to record video testimonies from Holocaust survivors and other witnesses.

8 The Winthrop Rockefeller Foundation, L'Oreal USA Inc., and the Jewish Federation of Arkansas provided the funding for the coordinator position in Arkansas. Arkansas was the third location nationwide chosen to launch the Testimony to Tolerance Initiative. Des Moines, Iowa, and Jackson, Mississippi, were the first two locations selected.

chapter ten

BRANCHING OUT

"In a sense, libraries are having to do what banks have done—go into the branch business."

BOBBY ROBERTS, 1989

The Central Arkansas Library System was already in the branch business when Roberts, speaking shortly after beginning his tenure as director, made the above statement. At that time, CALS had the Jacksonville, Sherwood, Perryville, Southwest, Fletcher, and Terry branches. With the exception of the Terry Branch, these locations grew out of requests from communities that were being served by the bookmobiles and from ad hoc library efforts.

A press release issued on February 12, 1990, announced that bookmobile service would stop at the end of February. The vehicles were in poor condition, and usage had dropped off for several years as branches opened. Ironically, the popularity of the bookmobiles eventually led to the demise of the program as demand for service had been the catalyst to develop branches in those communities. With the exception of a vehicle funded by a grant from Microsoft in the mid-1990s that took computer terminals into the communities, the era of the bookmobile was over.

Michael Brooks, who drove one of the bookmobiles during its last eight years of service, remembered, "People were really sorry to see it go. One woman said 'Didn't you stand up for us with the board?' I said, 'Ma'am, I'm so far down the line, I don't even think the board knows I'm here.'" On the last day of service, patrons showed their appreciation to Brooks with thank-you cards and going-away gifts.

Roberts knew that questions of where to build future branches and how to structure them, including both building design and programming, would be part of the conversation in any millage or bond issue elections. He saw the people in

Library staff members pose with the bookmobile on its last day of service.

the communities of Central Arkansas not only as potential library patrons but also as voters who would decide on funding issues. Roberts's arrival at CALS marked a shift from *reacting* to public demand to proactively *planning* for a system of branches serving all areas and being visible in each community.

Technology Improves Branches

To fully understand how far CALS has come during Roberts's time as director, examination must be given to how developing technology changed the face of library service.

In 1989, each branch functioned largely as a freestanding mini-library. Each one had a card catalog that itemized only the holdings of that branch. Patrons looking for books that were not available at the local branch either had to visit all the other branches or fill out paperwork requesting that the library try to find a copy of the books through interlibrary loan.

Until the library joined the OCLC network, locating books outside of the system presented quite a challenge. Linda Bly remembers taking requests over to the State Library to look up titles in the National Union Catalog, which consisted of huge bound volumes of photographs of library catalog cards from across the country.[1] She says she would have to browse through the books until she could find a library with the requested title.

Investing in automation in the 1990s allowed CALS to link all of the branches into a network with a single, comprehensive online catalog that allowed patrons to see what materials were available throughout the system. Books from anywhere in the system could be requested and picked up at the local branch and returned just as conveniently. The library maintenance staff began making pick-up and delivery runs to the branches on a regular basis, which cut down on the amount of time patrons had to wait to receive their materials.

The Internet also changed many aspects of library service. In the early 1990s reference librarians could access a computer program called InfoTrac that used CD-ROMs that contained updated periodical indices—a huge advance from having to wait for the indices to be compiled and published in print form. But, even that advancement in technology meant that each branch had to have a set of CDs. Today, the library invests more than $200,000 a year in subscriptions to online databases that are accessible from every branch, and, in many cases, from patrons' homes.

The Human Factor

Many people believed that the public library would become road kill on the information superhighway. Instead, CALS has embraced new technologies and found ways to integrate them into the library's service model. Books-on-tape morphed into books-on-CD—and now are starting to be replaced by download-able books. Reference librarians who turned to shelves of printed resources learned how to best use search engines and databases and how to evaluate the reliability of the myriad websites available.

As much as the landscape of library service has changed, making a personal connection with the public has not changed significantly since the day the Little Rock Public Library opened in 1910.

This human factor can be seen in the story-teller who holds the children's interest at story time; the public speakers who talk about critical, interesting, and sometimes funny topics; the person at the circulation desk who gives a pleasant greeting; the reference librarian who answers yet one more strange question; or the computer lab supervisor who helps a patron figure out how to print a résumé.

Each library branch is special to the area it serves. The staff has a greater opportunity to become part of the community and establish personal relationships with patrons. They learn about the unique needs of the neighborhoods and work to provide services that will enhance the community.

Melinda Jackson, the east zone manager for CALS, said, "Each of our branches is slightly different, and they reflect—to a certain extent—the community that they serve. You always have to keep that in mind. They are not identical. They don't serve identical groups of people, and they don't have identical needs. Their usership is different. What will work in one branch may not work in another branch because the needs and the interests are different."

For example, branches in lower-income neighborhoods may need to have more computer services available because the residents are less likely to have high-speed Internet connections in their homes. The librarians may spend more time showing patrons how to fill out on-line job applications than answering reference questions.

Jamie Melson, who started her career with CALS at the Jacksonville branch in 1979, said, "It is a totally different world. You are the provider of everything. Here at Main, we have the circulation desk, we have the reference department, we have the genealogy department...At the branches, you do the story time, you do the circulation, you do the reference—if the trash needs to be picked up, you do the trash."

Librarians who have served at CALS branches also speak of the personal relationships they developed with patrons. Linda Bly said, "You knew when a new book came in that Mrs. So-and-so would want to read it."

What Our Patrons Say

Responses to an informal patron survey conducted in 2009 show that public opinion of the library remains high.

"The library has allowed me to explore different types of literature, excel in my university studies and research, and allowed me to indulge my love of books without breaking the bank!"

"I love going to the library—people are always helpful and seem genuinely happy to help me find whatever obscure thing I'm looking for."

"I spent most of my time in my younger years in the bookmobile, as my mother worked full time and there wasn't time to get me to the library as often as I wanted. I am very thankful the bookmobile stopped in my neighborhood! All of the children looked forward to it."

"CALS has become a fabulous resource for our family, and we are very thankful for it. It has continued to foster a love of lifelong learning in our family that reaches across several generations. Thompson Library has grown into a neighborhood center for us, and we frequent it more often than we do the grocery store!"

"All my library visits are great...at all branches, but there's something incredible about Dee Brown. I live in Gravel Ridge but make a special trip to Dee Brown at least once a week. My son and I feel very welcome!"

"My sisters and I always looked forward to the bookmobile days. We didn't know you could ask for special titles so we just checked out what was there. Even in that cramped space, the smell of books was great. We had maybe five books and a set of World Books that we owned in our home. The access to books, especially during the summer, was invaluable."

"What I remember most is a particular book of fairytales in the children's section. There were low shelves arranged perpendicular to some windows, and it was second shelf from the bottom on a shelf in the middle of the rows of shelves. It was a thick, old book of fairytales with the most beautiful illustrations I've ever seen, even since. Nothing modern compares to the intricacy of those illustrations. I checked that book out over and over."

"When I moved here in 1988 after living in Memphis forty years, there were so many adjustments. CALS was a warm and inviting place, and I count the library as one of the first places in Little Rock where I 'settled' in to the community."

"I take my child to the Main Library and to Sanders in Sherwood. We have enjoyed many summer reading clubs together, and he loves to sit in front of the big windows in the children's area of the Main Library and read a book. Not only do we enjoy books, but we've seen animals, eaten bugs, and enjoyed magic shows, sing-a-longs, and puppet shows. Recently, I taught him to use the microfilm, and he was very excited to look up the days that we were born. There is always something interesting at the library."

Friends of the Central Arkansas Libraries

All aspects of CALS have benefited from the largess of the FOCAL organization, but none more than the library branches. Money raised at the periodic FOCAL book sales and through River Market Books & Gifts (CALS's "gently read" used bookstore) provides funds to support a variety of library needs: branch programming efforts, kits for book clubs with multiple copies of popular books and discussion information that can been checked out, the Summer Reading Club, the Read to Me program that provides books to newborns and toddlers, and many others. In 2009, FOCAL donated close to $50,000 to CALS. Margaret Yates said, "They have been very supportive through the years, more so now than ever."

Each branch manager selects a person from the community to represent that branch on the FOCAL board. Those representatives, along with the at-large members, serve as the governing body for the 1,100-member organization.

CALS also has friends in the wide variety of volunteers who give time to the library system—more than 11,500 hours in 2009. Melinda Jackson gave an example of one volunteer at the Fletcher Branch: "When I went to Fletcher, Hilda Coats would sit at the end of the circulation desk, pull the cards for the fiction books, and check them in every afternoon. She was in her eighties at the time. And, until the time we moved into the new building, she worked almost every day...She'd chat with her friends and people she didn't know. She was sitting right by the new fiction books and would say 'Oh, you ought to read that one; this is a great book.' She called it her 'selling books.' She was just a delight."

FOCAL volunteers have given thousands of hours of service to sort books and manage periodic book sales that benefit the library.

Bricks and Mortar

The first branches of CALS consisted of libraries that had been built as part of the Pulaski–Perry County Library or make-shift locations. The Terry Library in west Little Rock exemplified the direction the library was moving, as the Board of Trustees and the public saw what a library branch could be. CALS branches have won awards both from community organizations and from architectural design organizations. Each has been designed to fit into the community it serves and to meet that community's unique needs.

The following sections give brief histories of each building (branches and additions to the Main Library campus). Some of the branches have had multiple names and locations; those changes are noted in the headings of each section. They are listed in the order of earliest construction, beginning with the original Carnegie library building.

DESIGN
Polk, Stanley, Yeary;
Witsell, Evans, and Rasco;
and Cromwell Firm

CONSTRUCTION
Flynco, Inc.

AWARDS
1998 Award of Excellence—
Associated Builders and
Contractors

2002 Landscape Award,
Voluntary Upgrade—
Little Rock City Beautiful
Commission

2004 Award of Merit—
Quapaw Quarter Association

Main Library (1910, 1964, 1997)

700 LOUISIANA STREET (1910, 1964)
100 SOUTH ROCK STREET (1997)

The original Little Rock Public Library building, designed by Edward Tilton,[2] featured a grand façade with classical columns, moldings, and arches. Tilton's libraries during this period pioneered the "open plan," which involved placing the more popular books on open shelves where the public could access them freely instead of having all of the books stored in closed stacks where only the librarians could access them.

Local architect Charles Thompson oversaw the execution of Tilton's design, and the building opened to the public on February 1, 1910.

During the 1960s, the original Carnegie-funded building fell victim to the urban renewal movement. The City of Little Rock replaced the classical design of the library with modern design that incorporated many of the architectural elements popular during the 1960s. The exterior featured concrete "grillwork," and this grillwork motif was echoed inside the building to divide the public areas of the first floor from the administrative area. Many years later, Linda Bly met the contractor who worked on the building, and he told her that the concrete decorative grill was not the original pattern the architects had chosen. He said they started installing the original pattern and realized that it looked too much like swastikas, so they had to choose a different design. He told Bly that the original grill materials ended up on a motel in West Memphis.

The layout and construction of the building left little room for growth, and the thick plaster walls made adding new electrical outlets and telephone lines virtually impossible, which severely limited the amount of new technology that could be incorporated into the library. Only the director and the head of cataloging had private offices. Bly remembers that when she and Bob Razer became assistant directors, they had to squeeze two desks into the reception area outside of the director's office for their "offices."

The architects added an auditorium to the structure on the west side of the building. This room was named the Darragh Center for Intellectual Freedom in honor of Fred Darragh, who championed many social issues in Little Rock during his lifetime.

The top of the building is encircled with a frieze that features the names of authors ranging from Aristotle to Dr. Seuss. The library held an election to select these names, which were nominated and voted on by the general public.

When the Carnegie library was demolished, library patron Carl Martin saved the pillars that had stood at the entrance. When he saw them lying in the grass in front of the building, he simply asked the foreman for them.[3] Forty-five years later, Martin's family donated those same pillars back to the library, and they were erected in front of the Main Library at the west end of the parking lot in 2009 as part of the Carl and Lorene Martin Plaza.

The original Little Rock Public Library building.

The "remodel" of the Carnegie library transformed the look of the library into the typical urban-renewal architecture of the 1960s.

DESIGN
Witsell, Evans, and Rasco

CONSTRUCTION
Wilkins Construction

AWARDS
2009 Bronze Award—
American Society of Interior
Designers, South Central
Chapter

Esther Dewitt Nixon Library (1959, 1969, 2009)
Formerly known as the Jacksonville Library

CITY HALL, JACKSONVILLE (1959)

308 W. MAIN STREET, JACKSONVILLE (1969)

703 W. MAIN STREET, JACKSONVILLE (2009)

The Jacksonville area first received library service from the Pulaski County Library through its bookmobile service. Demand for service increased greatly during World War II when the Arkansas Ordnance Plant opened in Jacksonville, and again when the Little Rock Air Force Base opened in 1955.

Efforts to establish a full-service branch began in 1957 under the leadership of a city library commission, and Jacksonville opened its first public library inside city hall on November 22, 1959. This branch operated as a cooperative effort between the City of Jacksonville and the Pulaski County Library.

A bond issue approved by the voters in 1967 allowed $82,000 for the construction of a new library. This new, 10,000-square-foot building opened for service on March 17, 1969. This library became part of the Central Arkansas Library System in 1975 when the Pulaski–Perry County Library merged with the Little Rock Public Library.

Shelf-moving equipment can lift and transport fully loaded ranges of books.

The Jacksonville library underwent a facelift in the early 1990s, including new paint, new carpet, and reupholstering the furniture. Jamie Melson remembers that Bobby Roberts borrowed some prisoners from the city jail to help move the books. He rented large shelf-moving equipment that lifted entire ranges of shelves so that they could be rolled to a different part of the building without the books having to be boxed up and unloaded. Melson recalled that some of the ranges got mixed up when they moved them back into place, so the books in the fiction section were out of order and had to be rearranged by hand.

In 1992, the library renamed the building the Esther Dewitt Nixon Library in honor of the librarian who served as the branch manager from its inception until her retirement in 1986.

The Esther Dewitt Nixon Library, circa 1990s.

The library moved to a new, 13,500-square-foot building in 2009 that was constructed after Jacksonville voters approved a one-mill tax increase. The grand opening was held on February 14, 2009.[4]

Max Milam Library, Perryville (1961, 1993)

COURTHOUSE SQUARE (1961)

609 APLIN AVENUE, PERRYVILLE (1993)

DESIGN
Polk, Stanley, Saunders
& Associates

CONSTRUCTION
Gossett Construction

This branch originated in 1961 when citizens of Perry County approached the Pulaski County Library about forming a regional library after such alliances were sanctioned by state law.

The Perry County Library opened for business on December 3, 1961. The county received funding for the building but not for equipment and furnishings. The Winthrop Rockefeller Charitable Trust provided a grant to cover those costs.

By 1990, the Perry County Library operated with only $12,000 generated by property taxes. The rest of the library's budget came from state aid, county appropriations, and CALS support.

Perry County voters had approved a one-mill tax for library services in 1960, but Amendment 59 rolled back the level to 0.4 mill in 1980. The rural nature of the county and the fact that much of the land in the county belonged to the National Forest Service, which paid no property taxes, left the county without a solid tax base to support the library.

In 1990, the CALS Board of Trustees decided to develop a Model Rural Library in Perry County. The board promised to find funds for a new building if the county passed an operations millage. In November 1990, Perry County voters rejected every amendment on the ballot except the library millage, which passed by 54 percent of the vote.

In 1991, the Winthrop Rockefeller Trust donated $250,000 toward the construction of a new library building in Perryville. The gift was given in honor of Max Milam, a Perry County native who had served as director of finance and administration for governors Winthrop Rockefeller and Dale Bumpers, and also had served for a number of years as a trustee of the Rockefeller Trust. Milam was a tireless promoter for rural healthcare delivery and rural economic development in Perry County and around Arkansas, and the library board chose to name the new library after him.

The Library Services and Construction Act, gifts from the Sturgis Foundation, and funds transferred from CALS provided additional funding for the new building, which opened in July 1993.

The original Perry County library was housed in a small cinderblock building on the courthouse square. This 900-square-foot building served the community for more than 30 years.

DESIGN
Morris-Farrar Architects

CONSTRUCTION
Flynco, Inc.

Amy Sanders Library (1973, 1989)
Formerly known as the Sherwood City Library

510 SHERWOOD AVENUE, SHERWOOD (1973)
31 SHELBY DRIVE, SHERWOOD (1989)

Sherwood, originally a farming community located in northern Pulaski County, grew from a community of 714 in 1948 into a city of more than 28,000 in 2008. As the population grew, interest in library services outpaced what could be provided by visits from the Pulaski County bookmobile.

In 1973, the city, in cooperation with the Pulaski–Perry County Regional Library, opened the Sherwood City Library in a 600-square-foot building that had originally served as city hall.

In 1988, the Sherwood City Council approved plans to build a new, 9,000-square-foot library at the corner of Thornhill and Shelby Drive, and voted to name it in honor of longtime city clerk Amy Sanders. The building was funded with $143,000 from CALS and $314,000 from the City of Sherwood.

The new library opened to the public on February 14, 1989.

The Sanders facility moved just a few blocks, but the difference in the buildings was significant.

John Gould Fletcher Library (1974, 1996)

H STREET AT BUCHANAN (1974)

823 NORTH BUCHANAN STREET (1996)

The Fletcher Library grew out of recommendations made by Metroplan as part of a study conducted for the library in 1973. Metroplan's study, based on population figures and bookmobile circulation, recommended moving quickly to provide branch library service in the northwest portion of the city. Bookmobile service could be concentrated in the southwest part of the city—but a branch would soon be needed in that part of town also.

This branch opened in September 1974 in a renovated doctor's office at H and Buchanan streets and was named in memory of John Gould Fletcher, a Little Rock poet who won the Pulitzer Prize for poetry in 1937. This 6,000-square-foot building was purchased for $183,000.

The grand opening, originally planned for August, had been delayed for a month when the library learned the shelving would not be delivered on time. The shelving company notified the library of a second delay in delivery. The library did not want to delay the opening of the much-anticipated branch, so the staff lined up all of the books on the floor with the spines up and proceeded to open the branch. All of the books had to be moved again when the shelving arrived a week or so later.

The new branch brought a full-service library to a community and quickly replaced the need for the volunteer-driven Panhellenic Children's Library that had operated in the area for almost twenty years. In 1974, the Panhellenic Association transferred its equipment and collection to the new branch library, along with a check for $2,781 to help pay for furniture in the children's section of the new library.

In 1996, the library moved to its current location, directly behind the old location. The new, 13,500-square-foot building, which was built in the Craftsman style of design to blend in with the surrounding neighborhood, opened on May 4, 1996. CALS demolished the old building to make room for more parking.

DESIGN
AMR Architects

CONSTRUCTION
Robinette-Burnette Construction

AWARDS
1996 Design Award— American Institute of Architects, Arkansas Chapter

The original Fletcher Branch.

DESIGN
Fennell-Purifoy Architects

CONSTRUCTION
Flynco, Inc.

AWARDS
2002 Honor Award—
American Institute of
Architects, Arkansas Chapter

2002 Member Choice Award—
American Institute of Architects,
Arkansas Chapter

2002 Gold Award—American
Society of Interior Designers,
South Central Chapter

The Southwest City Mall provided a
high-traffic opportunity for the library.

WORLD RECORD

To raise public awareness and funds for a new library branch, local students David Bibb and Allen Wilder suspended themselves from the rafters of Southwest City Mall and embarked on a swinging marathon in an attempt to set a new world record. The pair remained aloft for 192 hours, which broke the previous *Guinness Book of World Records* mark of 182 hours.

Dee Brown Library (1976, 1979, 2002)
Formerly known as the Southwest Library

INTERSTATE 30 AND GEYER SPRINGS ROAD (1976)
5702 DREHER LANE (1979)
6325 BASELINE ROAD (2002)

By 1976, the bookmobile that serviced the southwest part of the city made two trips a week and accounted for 26 percent of the library's total circulation. CALS opened a storefront "unit" inside the Southwest City Mall to serve this growing population. This storefront branch proved to be extremely popular, and local efforts began immediately to help fund a permanent location.

The board selected a site directly behind the mall on Dreher Lane, and construction began. Student groups went door to door to raise funds for fixtures inside the new library, which opened for business behind the mall on August 6, 1979. The building had been deemed "substantially complete," so Rosemary Martin gave the go-ahead to begin service to the area. The formal dedication occurred on September 23, 1979.

The current building, located adjacent to the Southwest Little Rock Community Center, opened on March 9, 2002. The 13,500-square-foot building is named for Arkansas author and former librarian Dee Brown, who is best known for his 1970 book *Bury My Heart at Wounded Knee*. Little Rock artist Kevin Kresse created a bust of Brown that is located in a plaza in front of the building.

Brown, an apt choice to be honored, said at the branch dedication, "Whatever benefit I may ever have been to anybody in this world, much of the credit must go to a small library on Louisiana Street in Little Rock during the 1920s and 1930s. I first entered that library one day in 1924, a green sixteen-year-old just removed from then almost bookless south Arkansas. This teen-ager was hungry for information that might better his poor position in life, and for tales of faraway and romantic places. That small public library set me upon the road I would follow for a lifetime."

Adolphine Fletcher Terry Library (1990; 2001 [expansion])
2015 NAPA VALLEY DRIVE

Financed with $1.9 million in municipal bonds approved by voters in 1987 as part of a $39 million capital improvement package, the Terry Branch was the first to reflect the Board of Trustees' commitment to quality in all areas of the building.

The branch, which opened on April 28, 1990, was named for Adolphine Fletcher Terry, a trustee of the LRPL for forty years. Terry—a proponent of advancing Arkansas's school systems—helped develop the first school improvement association in the state.

The original building, the first CALS branch to receive an AIA award, covered 14,000 square feet; in 2000, an addition was begun to provide more public and administrative space and bring the building size to 19,030 square feet.

The Board of Trustees wanted the library to have a home-like feel, so they had the architects include a wood-burning fireplace. Shortly after Terry opened, the library installed gas logs, but the fireplace never caught on as a functional feature of the branch. The fireplace nook became a small meeting room during the 2001 expansion project.

DESIGN
Polk, Stanley & Associates Architects

CONSTRUCTION
Flynco, Inc.

AWARDS
1989 Interior Design Award—*Arkansas Times*

1990 Design Award—American Institute of Architects, Arkansas Chapter

DESIGN
Nathaniel, Curtis,
Riddick, Heiple
Architects

CONSTRUCTION
Hensel-Phelps
Construction

Aerospace Library (1995)

3301 EAST ROOSEVELT ROAD

Until 1995, the east side of Little Rock, which includes the communities of Wrightsville, Sweet Home, Granite Mountain, College Station, East End, and the Little Rock National Airport area, was served by a library station located in the East Little Rock Community Center, which closed in 1986. A bookmobile served the area until 1990.[5]

When the Aerospace Education Center was constructed near the airport, CALS created a unique branch within the larger facility. The branch opened on June 10, 1995, as part of the Aerospace Education Center. The center also includes an aerospace museum, an IMAX Theater, and a branch post office.

Because of the specific focus of the Aerospace Education Center, this branch was selected to house the Jay Miller Aviation History Collection, one of the world's most significant aviation and aerospace reference libraries. The collection includes approximately 6,000 books, 50,000 journals and magazines, 650 linear feet of manuscripts, and 350,000 photographs.

In December 2009, the Arkansas Supreme Court ruled that Pulaski County had prematurely applied a property tax increase, which meant that CALS could have to refund up to $1.5 million in taxes. In anticipation of having to refund some or all of the tax money, the Board of Trustees analyzed the entire library system to see where cost-saving measures could be taken. CALS implemented a hiring freeze and other cost-saving measures. The board decided to close the Aerospace Branch because its usage numbers had dropped significantly—only 2 percent of CALS's system-wide circulation came from that branch, and attendance at the branch had dropped by 12 percent, largely due to the declining population base in that service area.

The Aerospace Branch closed on May 26, 2010.

Maumelle Library (1996, 2007 [expansion])

10 LAKE POINTE DRIVE, MAUMELLE

The community of Maumelle opened a small library in the canteen room of the Community Center that offered limited hours on Tuesdays and Thursdays. This library developed as an expansion of the bookmobile service being provided by CALS.

Maumelle, which incorporated as a city in 1985, had its own Friends of the Library organization, which worked with CALS to construct a permanent library. Maumelle voters approved a $1 million bond issue in 1993 to finance construction.

Groundbreaking for the Maumelle Library was held on Valentine's Day of 1995, and the library opened on February 3, 1996.

This library, located near the walking path around Lake Valencia, has an interesting "green" feature. It is heated and cooled by a water-source, heat-pump HVAC system that uses Lake Valencia as the heat sink. The near-constant temperature of the lake has reduced the energy consumption of the library by approximately 35 percent over a conventional HVAC system.

The original 8,500-square-foot branch was expanded with a 3,535-square-foot addition in 2007.

DESIGN
Fennell Purifoy Architects

CONSTRUCTION
Flynco, Inc.

AWARDS
1997 Gulf States Regional Award—American Institute of Architects, Arkansas Chapter

1998 Honor Award—American Institute of Architects, Arkansas Chapter

DESIGN
Architecture
Innovations
Group

CONSTRUCTION
L. R. Mourning
Construction

Sue Cowan Williams Library (1997)

1800 CHESTER STREET

The Sue Cowan Williams Library is located across the street from the historic Dunbar High School (now the Dunbar Middle School). The branch is named for an African-American teacher who became well known when, in 1942, she filed a class-action lawsuit against the Little Rock School District for paying black teachers less than their white counterparts. Williams lost the case in the Arkansas courts, but her attorney—future U.S. Supreme Court justice Thurgood Marshall—appealed the decision in the U.S. District Court, Western Division, and won.

Architect Ron Bene Woods incorporated design elements of the exterior of Dunbar School (where Williams taught) into the exterior of the 8,500-square-foot building.

The branch opened on March 22, 1997.

Cox Creative Center (2001)

120 COMMERCE STREET

The Cox Creative Center is located on the Main Library campus in downtown Little Rock and serves as CALS's used bookstore, gift shop, and café. The oddly shaped building, once home to Cox Machinery Company, was acquired when CALS purchased the land that now is the Main parking lot. The building was constructed in 1906, and its shape follows the curving line of the railroad track that ran behind it.

The 18,000-square-foot building was renovated in 2001, and it served as the location of the library's exhibit and retail art galleries until 2009 when the art program moved to the new Arkansas Studies Institute. The Cox Center also houses River Market Books & Gifts, the library's "gently read" used bookstore. After the art program moved, the retail book and gift space expanded. The building also houses a small sandwich/coffee shop and A Thousand Words, a gallery exhibit of art work by CALS staff members.

DESIGN
Stocks-Mann Architects in association with Jameson Architects

CONSTRUCTION
Flynco, Inc.

AWARDS
2002 Bronze Award— American Society of Interior Designers, South Central Chapter

DESIGN
Stocks-Mann Architects

CONSTRUCTION
Flynco, Inc.

AWARDS
2006 Gold Award—
American Society
of Interior Designers,
South Central Chapter

Sidney S. McMath Library (2004)

2100 JOHN BARROW ROAD

The Sidney S. McMath Library, located in the west-central portion of Little Rock, sits on a ten-acre lot and includes a stocked pond and a nature trail. In addition to the 10,700-square-foot library facility, the CALS landscape department has a shop and a plant-holding area located on the grounds.

The branch is named for Sidney Sanders McMath, the first of Arkansas's modern progressive governors. A life-size statue of McMath waving his hat, created by Bryan Massey of Conway, greets visitors as they enter the library grounds.

This branch, which opened on December 4, 2004, offered CALS its first opportunity to expand the library's mission beyond the walls of the building by incorporating outdoor amenities for the public's use.

Roosevelt Thompson Library (2004)

38 RAHLING CIRCLE

DESIGN
AMR Architects

CONSTRUCTION
Alessi Keys
Construction

The Roosevelt Thompson Library, located in the northwest portion of Little Rock, opened on September 25, 2004.

This branch includes a courtyard that serves as an outdoor reading room and program room where patrons can enjoy the fountain and bog pond located on the property.

The 13,500-square-foot facility is named for Roosevelt Thompson, the 1980 valedictorian at Central High School, who had achieved the highest score ever by an Arkansan on the National Merit Scholarship exam. Thompson was attending Yale University and preparing to receive a Rhodes scholarship when he died in a car crash in March 1984.

DESIGN
Polk Stanley Rowland
Curzon Porter Architects,
Ltd.

CONSTRUCTION
East-Harding Construction

AWARDS
2009 Award of Merit—
Quapaw Quarter
Association

2009 Judges Award for
Construction—South
Central Construction

2009 Silver Award—
American Society of
Interior Designers,
South Central Chapter

2009 Honor Award—
American Institute of
Architects, Gulf States

2009 Honorable Mention
(New Construction in a
Historic Setting)—Historic
Preservation Alliance of
Arkansas

continued

Arkansas Studies Institute (2009)

401 PRESIDENT CLINTON AVENUE

Construction of the Arkansas Studies Institute (ASI) presented CALS with its most challenging project, and prompted Bobby Roberts to jokingly declare "no more old buildings."

Located on the Main Library campus in downtown Little Rock, the ASI combines architecture from three different centuries in its 65,746 square feet. The project preserved two historic buildings for adaptive reuse and joined them with a new building to provide space for research materials, collection storage, meeting rooms, office space, and art galleries.

CALS purchased the Geyer & Adams building, home to Farrell & Schaer Blueprint Company, in September 2003. Roberts originally envisioned adding a glass structure to the west side of the building that would contain, among other things, the research room for the ASI. The concrete Geyer & Adams building would be used to store the combined archival collections of the Butler Center for Arkansas Studies and UALR's Archives and Special Collections.

The Geyer & Adams building's load test showed that it would not be able to bear the weight of the shelving and materials, so the architects had to rethink the plan and make the glass building the archival portion of the structure.

In November 2004, CALS learned that the revenue from a one-mill tax voters had approved renewing in August would bring in an additional approximately $3 million. The board used part of that money to purchase the Porbeck & Bowman building (also known as the Budget Office building), which abuts the Geyer & Adams building on the east side.

Linda Bly said, "The difficulty about this project was that the program was always changing. It was not like any other project that we worked on….For a branch, [we say] we're going to build a 14,000-square-foot building, and this is what it is going to do….The ASI building was in constant flux in terms of space use, program use…everything. And then when the buildings turned out to have issues that we didn't realize existed when we purchased them, then it made it that much more difficult to get a handle on what we were trying to do."

The issues with the buildings ranged widely. The Porbeck & Bowman building (built in 1882) did not have a solid foundation, and the entire south wall had to be taken down and rebuilt. The decorative stars on the east side of the building mask long bolts that hold up that wall. The floors in the Geyer & Adams building (built in 1914) did not have the load-bearing capacity anticipated. Also, the building sat over an underground spring that had flooded the basement. That water had corroded the iron and steel in the support columns, and the building had to be jacked up while the construction company rebuilt the supports.

The devastation from Hurricane Katrina in 2005 added to the construction delays at the ASI, as the cost of and lead time to receive all of the building materials increased due to the shortages caused by the demand in the Gulf area. In the end, the ASI took five and a half years to complete from the time the Geyer & Adams building was purchased.

The grand opening reception, which was held on March 22, 2009, included speeches by Arkansas governors Dale Bumpers, David Pryor, Jim Guy Tucker, Bill Clinton, and Mike Beebe.

The ASI has won more awards than any other CALS project—for design, construction, décor, and historic preservation.

Renovating two historic structures proved to be an architectural and construction challenge.

AWARDS CONT'D

2009 Excellence in Preservation through Rehabilitation—Historic Preservation Alliance of Arkansas

2009 Member's Choice Award—American Institute of Architects, Arkansas Chapter

2009 Decorative Project of the Year—Concrete Construction

2009 Best Overall in South Central Region—South Central Construction

2010 National Award—American Institute of Steel Construction

DESIGN
Allison Architects

CONSTRUCTION
James H. Cone, Inc.

Oley E. Rooker Library (projected 2010)

11 OTTER CREEK COURT

CALS broke ground on May 2, 2009, on a new library near the entrance to the Otter Creek subdivision in southwestern Little Rock. The 13,500-square-foot building is scheduled to open in the last quarter of 2010.

After compiling suggested names from the public, the Board of Trustees chose to name the new library after Oley Eldon Rooker, a manufacturer's representative for more than 40 years who was president of the Crystal Valley Property Owners Association and served as a strong advocate for the tax increase that made the new library possible.

The Rooker Library will be CALS's first LEED (Leadership in Energy and Environmental Design) certified "green" building, which means the design and orientation of the building and the materials used in its construction all work together to create a facility that is sensitive to the environment in its operations and maintenance requirements. A geothermal heating and cooling system, high-efficiency windows with strategically placed sun screens, and high-efficiency lighting are designed to work together to achieve both energy efficiency and good indoor environmental quality. The grounds feature a reflecting pool with sculptures depicting otters and a pavilion to accommodate outdoor programs and gatherings.

1 According to Wikipedia, "The Library of Congress began its union catalog project in 1901 in an attempt to locate and note the location of a copy of every important book in the United States. With financial assistance from John D. Rockefeller Jr., the collection grew to over 11 million cards. Copies of these cards were distributed to a number of libraries around the country. Eventually the cards for all materials catalogued by the cooperating libraries were reproduced and issued serially in printed volumes as the National Union Catalog, supplementing the Library of Congress Catalog of Printed Books. Monthly NUC catalogs were cumulated quarterly, annually, and multi-annually." Online at http://en.wikipedia.org/wiki/National_Union_Catalog (accessed July 6, 2010).

2 Edward Tilton specialized in designing libraries and other public buildings. His close friendship with James Bertram, Andrew Carnegie's personal secretary, garnered him many recommendations to be the architect of choice for Carnegie-funded libraries.

3 *Arkansas Democrat-Gazette*, February 4, 2002.

4 Nancy Dockter, "Jacksonville's New Library Is Open to Public," *The Leader*, February 16, 2009. Online at http://www.arkansasleader.com/2009/02/top-story-jacksonvilles-new-library-is.html (accessed July 10, 2010).

5 The East Little Rock Community Center was formed in 1973 as part of the Model Cities Program.

chapter eleven

THE VIEW AT 100:
FORWARD FROM HERE

"The battle over whether we survive as viable tools for the transmission of knowledge…depends entirely on our ability to convince society of the value of libraries."[1]

BOBBY ROBERTS

As CALS is poised on the edge of its second century of service, Bobby Roberts continues to think of new ways to integrate the library into the community as an agent for positive change. His current project, arguably his most ambitious, is the Children's Library initiative.

This library will be located in the midtown area north of 12th Street and east of Jonesboro Drive, an area that deteriorated significantly after the construction of Interstate 630. The Children's Library will combine traditional library services with a learning center where children and youth from all socio-economic groups can be exposed to a wide variety of learning opportunities. Much of the focus of the initiative is centered on partnering with other organizations that provide educational opportunities and developing new programs with these organizations. Don Ernst, who heads up the project, says the possibilities are endless. The library site could incorporate children's theater, art classes, vegetable plots where children can learn about agriculture as well as healthy eating, cooking classes…and on and on. Ernst explains that he wants the children to focus on the experience of learning without the pressure of being graded on knowledge or skills.

Roberts believes that this library can help reverse some of the damage that construction of the interstate inflicted on the neighborhoods south of the interstate. Plans for developing the library and its campus overlap with the city's plans to extend War Memorial Park to the south over the interstate. These two initiatives are expected to encourage the revitalization of the adjacent 12th Street corridor.

"At the moment that we persuade a child, any child, to cross that threshold, that magic threshold into a library, we change their lives forever, for the better." Keynote speaker Senator Barack Obama made this statement at the 2005 American Library Association's annual conference.

Roberts also dreams of having a major research library located in Little Rock, perhaps on the order of the Science, Industry, and Business Library that is part of the New York Public Library. He thinks that this type of library could be instrumental in the economic growth of Arkansas. The price tag is as big as the dream, however. He estimates that such a library would cost $100 million—a not-so-small roadblock; of course, he is already calculating how the library could accomplish this dream: "If I could wave my magic wand and pass this last millage of taxes,[2] we'd have more than $42 million dollars; that would get you forty-five percent of what you needed."

Patrons are not the only ones who give rave reviews to the staff of the library. Many of the current employees decided to become librarians because of their experiences in the public library, and many long-term library employees cite the influence of their supervisors and mentors in developing their library skills. When asked to talk about some of the people who mentored or inspired them, they responded enthusiastically.

"Stacy Plant and John McGraw were my first supervisors here, and they both seemed to carry themselves with an air of professionalism that no angry patron could ruffle."

"Jim Hicks…had such a good work ethic and taught me a lot about reference sources."

"Peggie Machen was probably one of the best supervisors I've ever had. She was patient, answered questions without making me feel silly, and seemed to take most everything calmly. She worked hard and set a great example. It was always easy to give her the respect she deserved."

"Kate Matthews and Terri Bailey know how to balance CALS procedures with the reality of patrons…Library-land in theory verses reality are two very different things, and they know how to make it work."

"Bettye Kerns is one of those people who makes juggling six projects look easy. I've learned a lot from Bettye about handling all types of situations."

"Ever since my first day of work at Dee Brown, Sarah McClure has made me feel so loved and welcome. Sarah is the reason I'm starting library school in the fall. She's an amazing librarian, and now I want to be, too."

"Alice Gray just had the most courage. She had cancer; it just kept coming back in different places. I remember one time when I happened to be at the circulation desk when she came down the hall from her office, and she was just barely making it—until she got within sight of people. Then, she pulled it all together and marched out just like a queen. I don't think anyone was ever a malingerer or took a sick day when they weren't really sick. She led by example."

"Esther Dewitt Nixon was a Renaissance woman who had a dream of what the library could be. She devoted her adult life to developing an institution that offered a world of possibilities to those who entered its doors. Esther loved to talk about books and writers and encouraged readers to be passionate about their favorites."

"Esther Nixon was a true Southern lady—quiet, reserved, polite, genteel. She knew everybody in Jacksonville. She knew how to approach the people. She knew how to talk to the people. When there was a problem, she knew how to handle it…That library was her baby."

"When I was in high school, I got a job as a page at the Terry Branch. Hames Ware was my supervisor, and he was very instrumental in ensuring that I returned to CALS after graduating from college. In addition to giving us guidance in work-related matters, he was always ready with an encouraging word about matters outside of work."

"Stacy Plant began her career with CALS as a page and worked her way up [to assistant manager of the circulation department]. She was the most compassionate boss I've ever had. She once spent an hour talking me through boyfriend problems so that I could stop crying and do my job. She worked here through many illnesses, including a brain tumor, as well as the death of her best friend, Kristi Buss. She never let her troubles interfere with her professionalism or her caring attitude."

"Linda Bly has an ability to look at situations in a really unique way. She always helped me to see ways to solve problems in a different direction than what I originally thought."

"Bobby Roberts is full of ideas, but he is also very detail-oriented. Bobby has got his finger on the pulse of everything we do, and he presents a great public persona—he is the face of the library. He is so tied to the library, and under his leadership the library has developed such a positive image in the community."

"Alice Coleman was the head of reference when I came here. My year of graduate school, I felt like, got me in the door and got me through my first day, and Alice taught me everything I knew after that."

"Louise Smith was such an inspiration to me—here was an African-American woman who was coming to work every day in her suits—well-dressed in her heels and things. And, it was just inspiring to me to have somebody I could look up to."

"Everybody that has come to the library for a long time will remember [security guard] Vernon Johnson because he was so larger than life—physically as well as in personality. He was just a fixture at the library; he would help anybody. One year, when we collected money for the cereal drive, he made a second donation and said, "I just can't stand the thought of hungry children.""

"Kristi Buss had a [breast cancer] relapse. She just had such a spirit about her that so many people were touched by watching how she conducted herself. She never complained; she always felt gratitude for the help we tried to give her. She never wanted to not come to work. It really changed a lot of people. If you want to set the bar high as far as dedication and an unwillingness to be a martyr or to wallow in your pain or your grief, Kristi would be the one you would look to."

Beyond Bricks and Mortar

No matter how many buildings Roberts envisions, he is quick to acknowledge that the real future of the library lies in the hands of the staff. He says that, above all, he hopes the library never loses its commitment to public service. "The best community tie we've always had is that the staff does a good job...We've always had a good public service model and a good public service attitude."

Jennifer Chilcoat explained that attitude of public service: "This is a public library, and people come in with every range of vulnerability and every range of need. They all deserve the best that we can offer them from where they are coming from. If we can accommodate them at all, we've got to find a way to step out and meet them where they are and to be helpful to them."

Technology Today and Tomorrow

CALS is in the middle of another major automation project—RFID tagging. Carol Coffey, who heads the RFID team, explained, "Radio Frequency Identification is a new way of allowing our books to communicate with the library catalog. Patrons walk into a library, take a book off the shelf, scan their library card, set the book on a computer pad, and it's checked out—they're done and ready to go. It allows patrons to protect their privacy; they don't have to have any staff interaction if they don't want to. It will allow us to keep a better inventory and to redeploy our staff so that they can do more to help patrons find what they are looking for."

Coffey continues to investigate new technology and ways it can be incorporated into library service. CALS recently invested in a service called Overdrive, which allows people to download electronic books for a two-week period. Coffey says that to remain viable, CALS must move toward the public demand for more resources that can be accessed with smart phones and other personal devices.

During the conversion to RFID tags, library staff will have to tag almost one million items.

These types of technology make library patrons much more self-sufficient. Melinda Jackson thinks the challenge that comes with this independence is making sure librarians remain connected with the patrons. She said, "When they had to come to the desk, we always had that interaction with them. We connected names with people because we had the constant interaction. It's going to be a little more challenging especially for the [patrons] who get very comfortable with self check. Being accessible and available to the patrons is going to be the challenge that we have."

Margaret Yates says the library of the future is going to have to be more in tune with the developing technologies. The library of the future may look very different, with fewer books on shelves and more table space for devices that can be used in the building. She said, "There will always be a segment of the community who does not have access to the latest technology, whatever that might be at that time. So, I still see the library as still playing a big role in getting whatever information in whatever form it may come in out [to the public]. Library professionals will still have to know the information and what's available out there, but they may be looking at it on an e-reader instead of in a book."

Coffey agrees that libraries will change and adapt, but she does not see them becoming obsolete: "So many of the really good materials are out there, but they are in these large databases that cost tens of thousands of dollars. The library becomes your gateway to get to this good stuff."

In Conclusion

The history of the Central Arkansas Library System can be summed up by one word: vision. From Andrew Carnegie's vision of making information readily available to the masses to Bobby Roberts's vision of the public library as an agent of social change, CALS has spanned 100 years of library revolution and development—from Carnegie to cyberspace and beyond.

---

1 This quote is extracted from an *Arkansas Libraries* article analyzing the effects of the 1980 presidential election for libraries in the state. Roberts wrote: "Traditionally, libraries have prospered only under activist governments that see libraries both as tools to serve the larger public welfare and as symbols of a mature, caring society. Conversely, we have fared poorly when government has looked on itself as merely a caretaker...The battle over whether we survive as viable tools for the transmission of knowledge...depends entirely on our ability to convince society of the value of libraries...To survive we must be ready to act politically in our own self-interest. It is the way of American politics." Bobby Roberts, "The Forum 1980: The End of the New Deal for Libraries?" *Arkansas Libraries* 38 (March 1981): 7–8.

2 The Arkansas constitution currently allows a total of three mills for capital expenditures; CALS is currently at two mills.

Appendices

Central Arkansas Library System
Policies and Statements

The CALS Board of Trustees' statements below reflect the library's philosophy of service to our communities, and these statements guide the operation of the library:

The Library's Vision

We shall be a primary public source of information in the central Arkansas area and shall provide access to that information to all who want it. Our circulation will continue to rise as our holdings grow and as we refine and keep current our collections. We shall be a leader in increasing the research resources necessary to assist in the community's economic and social development, and shall ourselves stay abreast of developments in information technology useful to our patrons and the community. Our public programming on regional history and culture will draw broad participation. The Library will be recognized by people in our service area as a lively, accessible, expert, user-friendly source of information.

The Library's Mission

To acquire, organize, and administer collections of books and related materials and to provide access and services that best meet the needs of our patrons for information and enjoyment.

The Library's Core Values

- We believe free public libraries are essential in a democratic society.

- We respect the dignity of our patrons and the diversity of their needs.

- We nurture the basic human attribute of curiosity and support the pursuit of adventure, discovery, knowledge, wisdom, and understanding.

- We defend vigorously the principles of intellectual and artistic freedom.

- We invest in our staff to enhance their abilities and encourage their enthusiasm to better serve the public.

The Library's Strategic Goals

- To preserve the heritage and history of the communities we serve, and to provide information on the governance, economic activity, and cultural opportunities of those communities.

- To stay abreast of the best of information technology and to make it available to our patrons and their communities.

- To add to and refine the library's holdings, facilities, and operational capacity in pursuit of our mission.

- To collaborate with other institutions in the interest of building strong communitywide information resources.

Librarians/Directors and Dates of Service

(Initially, the person in charge of the library or library system was referred to as the librarian and other employees were referred to as, for example, the reference librarian. The person in charge of the system later became known as the director.)

Little Rock Public Library (LRPL):

Mary Maud Pugsley (1910–1912)

Pugsley, of Boston, Massachusetts, served as librarian in Wheaton, Illinois, and as reference librarian at the Art Institute of Chicago before coming to Little Rock. She left Little Rock in December 1912 to accept a reference position at the Public Library in Newark, New Jersey.

Dorothy Dodd Lyon (1912–1918)

A native of Haverhill, Pennsylvania, Lyon had previously served as the children's librarian at the Cleveland Public Library. She joined the LRPL as children's librarian and was appointed librarian in December 1912. She served for several years as secretary for the Arkansas Library Association.

Beatrice Prall (1918–1926)

Prall, a native of Hope (Hempstead County), graduated from the University of Arkansas and the University of Illinois Library School before she joined the library staff in July 1916 as cataloger and general assistant. She was appointed librarian in 1918 and served until she retired and moved to Knoxville, Tennessee.

Vera Jessie Snook (1926–1948)

Snook was a native of Ottawa, Illinois. She came to Little Rock after serving libraries in Illinois and Montana. She earned both bachelor's and master's degrees from the University of Illinois. She then took one year of a two-year library training at the Illinois Library School, also at the University of Illinois, before leaving the school in 1913 for a teaching job in Tennessee.

After one year of teaching, Snook took a position as librarian at the Reddick Library in her home town of Ottawa, serving there from 1914 to 1922. As early as 1919, she felt she had accomplished all that she could in Ottawa and was looking for a position that would be more of a challenge. In 1922, she took a position at the Lincoln County Library in Libby, Montana, where she served until she came to Little Rock in 1926.

Catherine Thompson Chew (1948–1957)

Chew was born in Clarksburg, West Virginia, and moved to Little Rock with her family when she was ten. She graduated from high school in Little Rock in 1923, and received a BA from Wellesley College and a BS in library science from the University of Illinois. She also studied at the Carnegie Library School in Pittsburgh, Pennsylvania, which specialized in training children's librarians. She served as LRPL's children's librarian, 1929–1938; state supervisor of WPA library projects, 1938–1944; Pulaski County librarian, 1944–1946; desk assistant at LRPL, 1947–1948; and librarian, 1948–1957 (beginning in October 1955, she worked part time due to illness; she remained the official librarian until her death in April 1957). She was also president of the Arkansas Library Association during the 1940s.

Margaret Burkhead (1957–1969)

A native of St. Louis, Missouri, Burkhead attended Harris College and the Strassburger Conservatory of Music in St. Louis and Mount Holyoke College in Massachusetts, but she did not hold a degree. She moved to Little Rock in 1939 with her husband, who worked for Missouri Pacific Railroad. Burkhead worked for the United States Employment Service testing applicants for secretarial positions before she joined the LRPL as executive secretary, to oversee the bookkeeping and finances. She became administrator in October 1955 and director on April 18, 1957. Burkhead retired at the end of 1969.

Alice Newton Gray (1970–1978)

Gray, a native of Hope (Hempstead County), first worked for the LRPL as a page while she was a sophomore at Little Rock High School. Returning to Little Rock in 1950 with a degree in philosophy from the University of Arkansas, Gray worked part time at the library from 1950 to 1964, when she became reference librarian. In 1965, she became assistant director and also began pursuing a master's degree in library science from Columbia. She became director of the library in 1970. Gray remained as director until her death from cancer in May 1978.

In July 1980, the library established the Alice Newton Gray Memorial Fund in honor of the director. The fund was established from memorial gifts received in Gray's honor. Her family asked that the monies be used to provide a means for continuing education for staff members. The fund was used to provide educational loans, and the first two staff members to receive loans from the fund were Meredith May and Suzanne Druehl. By 1994, the fund had grown enough to provide outright scholarship grants instead of loans.

Rosemary Scarbrough Martin (1978–1989)

Martin, a native of Webster County, Mississippi, came to CALS in 1978 via the Dallas Public Library. Martin graduated from Mississippi State College for Women and received a master's degree in library science from the University of Wisconsin in Madison. Before joining the Dallas Public Library, she had been a librarian at the Memphis and Shelby County Public Library.

Bobby Roberts (1989–present)

A native of Helena (Phillips County) and a graduate of Central High School of Helena-West Helena, Roberts received a BS from the University of Central Arkansas in Conway, an MLS from the University of Oklahoma in Norman, and an MA and a PhD in history from the University of Arkansas in Fayetteville. A former campaign aide and legislative liaison for Governor Bill Clinton, Roberts also served on the board of the Arkansas Department of Correction, the Delta Cultural Board, and the State Review Committee for the Arkansas Historic Preservation Program. Roberts served as head of Archives and Special Collections at the University of Arkansas at Little Rock from 1978 until 1989, although he took several leaves of absence for Clinton-related projects.

Pulaski County Library:

Lois Ranier (1938–1940)

Ranier, from Troy, Alabama, came to the Pulaski County Library position after serving as librarian at the College of Engineering at the University of Arkansas in Fayetteville. She was a graduate of Alabama Teachers College and the University of Wisconsin Library School. She also did graduate work at the University of Chicago and had two years' experience in teaching and in school library work prior to joining the Pulaski County Library. Ranier left the Pulaski County Library on September 1, 1939, to become the state library consultant for WPA libraries in Alabama.

Gordon Bennett (1940–1942)

Bennett served libraries in Nebraska and Denver, Colorado, before coming to Little Rock in 1940; he left to accept a position as head of the West Virginia Library Commission.

Frances Clark (1942–1944)

A graduate of Texas University and of the Louisiana State University Library School, Clark served as an assistant with the Texas State Library before accepting the position as Pulaski County librarian. In 1944, she married Robert Bryson and left the Pulaski County Library.

Catherine Thompson Chew (1944–1946)

[See previous LRPL information.]

Mary Sue Shepherd (1946–1975)

Shepherd attended Hendrix College in Conway and received a bachelor's degree from a college in Colorado. She taught school in Pine Bluff and Pulaski County and also worked for the American Red Cross.

After the Pulaski–Perry County Regional Library consolidated with the Little Rock Public Library, Shepherd went to work at the Southwest Branch of CALS, where she stayed until her death in 1982.

Board of Trustees

CALS is a "public body corporate and politic," which means it is a public corporation whose assets are held in trust for the benefit of the public and is not a department or agency of the cities or counties in which it operates libraries. Its authority is established by Arkansas Code Annotated 13-2-502 Little Rock City Code, Section 16-26,27—Interlocal Agreement through which the participating governmental bodies cede their library authority to a single, thirteen-member Board of Trustees. This board is responsible for establishing all policies and services for the library system.

2010 Board of Trustees:

- Elgin Clemons Jr. (Little Rock)
- Gayle Corley (Little Rock)
- Jimmie Lou Fisher (Little Rock)
- Annette Herrington (Little Rock)
- Stanley Hill (Pulaski County)
- Beverly Masters (Maumelle)
- Jim Metzger (Pulaski County)
- Archie Moore Jr. (Little Rock)
- T. T. Tyler Thompson (Little Rock)
- Cheryl Vines (Sherwood)
- Laveta Wills-Hale (Little Rock)
- Tamara Walkingstick (Perry County)
- Mark Wilson (Jacksonville)

The following table lists all known trustees of the library. The names are drawn principally from published annual reports and Board of Trustees' minutes. Because record keeping was at times sketchy, the list may be incomplete; for the same reason, terms of service are sometimes uncertain or missing.

Mayor of LR, ex officio chairman	1907–1940
J. N. Heiskell	1907–1972
H. F. Auten	1907–1917
M. M. Cohn	1907–1920
George B. Rose	1907–1942
T. M. Bunch	1907–1917
Samuel Reyburn	1907–1917
T. M. Mehaffey	1910–1942
John M. Moore Sr.	1910–1920
Carl Voss	1910–1925
William S. Mitchell (Bd. of Public Affairs)	1913–1917
A. B. Poe (Bd. of Public Affairs)	1913–1917
Jacob Trieber	1920–1925
Robert M. Butterfield	1925
Lloyd England	1925
Charles T. Coleman	1920–1945
G. Coleman	1925
G. DeMatt Henderson	1920–1942
Adolphine Fletcher Terry	1926–1965
Rabbi Ira Sanders	1926–1977
Josephine M. Brown	1931–1942
Hilda Cornish	1931–1957
J. H. Hollis	1934–1935
J. S. Utley	1941
A. F. House	1945–1948
Shields M. Goodwin	1950–1955
G. W. Blankenship	1956–1957
Fred K. Darragh Jr.	1970–1980
Booker Worthen	1958–1979
Louise Vinson	1958–1969
Ginny Brown	1966–1979
Raymond Rebsamen	1973–1975
Clarice Miller	1974–1981
William Thompson	1974–1980
Ralph Patterson	1976–1981

Eleanor Reid	1978–1980
Verlon Stone	1978
Mrs. Mattie Kinchen	1978–1982
Shirley Lowery	1979–1980
Jo Ann Newell	1980–1982
Mary Ross Thomas	1980–1986
Ray Gabbard	1980–1982
Ruth N. Wilson	1981–1986
Johnny Biggs	1981–1982
Frederick J. Menz	1981–1986
Phil Anderson	1982–1987
Wanda Hamilton	1982–1987
John Kizer	1983–1984
Marsha Stewart	1983–1984
Marion Cullins Hegarty	1983–1985
Leland Gordon	1983–1989
Linda Goss Napper	1984–1990
Lunsford Bridges	1985–1989
Jane Moses	1986–1991
Sherry Walker	1986–1991
John McNee	1987–1992
Rick Campbell	1987–1992
Katherine Mitchell	1988–1993
Tom Dillard	1988–1996
William Terry	1990–1999
Betty Overton	1990
Joyce Wilson	1991–2004
Sherman Banks	1992–2002
Frances O. "Freddie" Nixon	1992–2002
Berniece Benjamin	1992–1996
Somers Matthews	1993–1996
Wally Nixon	1993–2004
David Rickard	1994–2005
Judith Faust	1996–2005
Shirley Pine	1996–2003
James McHaney	1997–2004
Fanye Porter	1999–2004
J. J. Lacey Jr.	1999–2004
Buddy Metcalf	1999–2002

Shirley Hale	1999–2000
Annette Herrington	2000–2012
Nan Gentry	2001–2002
Nate Coulter	2003–2008
Billy Jo Branscum	2003–2005
Lisa Ferrell	2003–2008
Sara Beth Dawson	2003–2009
Michel Leidermann	2004–2009
Mark Wilson	2005–2010
Beverly Masters	2005–2010
Jim Metzger	2005–2010
Joyce Elliott	2005–2007
T. T. Tyler Thompson	2005–2010
Jimmie Lou Fisher	2006–2011
Stanley Hill	2006–2011
Tamara Walkingstick	2006–2011
Elgin Clemons Jr.	2008–2010
Gayle Corley	2009–2011
Laveta Wills-Hale	2009–2011
Cheryl Vines	2010–2012
Archie Moore Jr.	2010–2012

Pulaski County Library and
Pulaski-Perry County Regional Library Trustees

Bessie Kahn	—
Alfred H. Craig	1938–1967
Sue K. George	1938–1945
Louise S. Moose	1938–1971
A. F. Henry	1938–1940
Samella Campbell	1938–1969
Thelma Isgrig	1938–1968
Walter Barron	1942
Dorothy Miller	1945–1954
J. L. Hudson	1951–1954
Harvey L. Young	1955–1964
Pat Wilson	1955–1969
Louise Schiffer	1965–1974
Ben C. Isgrig Jr.	1970–1974
J. L. Watson	1970–1974
Fred Bowen	1970–1974
Mrs. George Dortch-Scott	1970–1972
Emily C. Barrier	1972–1974
David Lyons	1973–1974

Staff Award Winners

Super Page

Pages provide a tremendous amount of support to the library's professional staff by handling numerous responsibilities, including reshelving books, checking in returned books, and aiding at the public service desks. Many people who chose to be professional librarians started their careers as pages.

1999	Guadalupe "Lupe" Pena	Southwest Branch
2000	Jennifer Swaty	Terry Branch
2001	Amanda Cartwright	Sanders Branch
2002	Suma Mellekatte	Main (Youth Services)
2003	Paul Belov	Main (Circulation)
2004	Julie Ludwig	Main (Circulation)
2005	Amber King	Dee Brown Branch
2006	Elizabeth Baker	Terry Branch
2007	Tiffany Braggs	Dee Brown Branch
2008	Robin Kanatzar	Terry Branch
2009	Rosa Gallman	Thompson Branch

Employee of the Year

Employee of the Year candidates are nominated by their peers, and the candidates are voted on by the entire staff of the library.

1983	Billye Sligh	Main (Cataloging)
1984	Melrita Bonner	Main (Circulation)
1985	Bette Kirk	Southwest Branch
1986	Peggie Machen	Main (Circulation)
1987	Almeta Smith	Main (Circulation)
1988	Eddie Swartout	Main (Security)
1989	Renee Grimes	Maintenance
1990	James Tillman	Maintenance
1991	Cherece Watson	Public Relations
	Margaret Coakley	Community Relations
1992	Bettye Kerns	Youth Services
	Larrie Thompson	Administration
1993	Raymond Ross	Maintenance
1994	Alysanne Crymes	Reference
1995	Scott James	Computer Services
1996	Tracy Hamby	Cataloging
1997	Tim Conrad	Maintenance
1998	Lilianna Czerniawska	Main (Cataloging)
1999	Audrey Taylor	Aerospace Branch
2000	Ellen Bard	Main (Computer Network Services)
2001	Mike Brooks	Main (Circulation)
2002	Leroy Bailey	Security
2003	Erica Robie	Main (Computer Network Services)
2004	John McGraw	Main (Circulation)
2005	Raleigh Peterson	Main (Reference)
2006	Terri Bailey	Main (Circulation)
2007	Rhonda Stewart	Main (Butler Center for Arkansas Studies)
2008	Jessie Clark-Nalley	Main
2009	Brian Martin	Dee Brown Branch

Unsung Hero

The unsung hero award recognizes people whose extraordinary contributions may not be known to the library staff at large. They are nominated by their fellow employees and selected by a panel of judges who review the narratives that accompany the nominations.

1994	Lawrence Gupton	Main (Housekeeping)
1995	Renee Grimes	Administration
1996	Terry Dwyer	Administration
1997	Ginann Swindle	Sanders Branch
	Peggy Machen	Main (Circulation)
1998	Meg Warren	Maumelle Branch
1999	Carolyn Lasseigne	Fletcher Branch
2000	David Edwin Gifford	Main (Reference)
2001	Almeta Smith	Southwest Branch
	Elizabeth Johnson	Southwest Branch
2002	Hames Ware	Terry Branch
2003	Eleanore Lipke	Main (Youth Services)
	Tim Phillips	Sanders Branch
2004	David Walls	Main (Reference)
2005	Nakisha Lindsey	Fletcher Branch
2006	Jan Guffey	Milam Branch
2007	Dawn Perry	Main (Computer Network Services)
2008	Shanna Howard	Nixon Branch
2009	Terri Bailey	Fletcher Branch

Library Awards Received by CALS Trustees and Staff

Board of Trustees members and CALS staff have been recognized by outside organizations for a variety of achievements. CALS maintains a plaque in the board room of the Main Library to record these honors.

1957	J. N. Heiskell	Trustee Citation; American Library Association
1980	Ida Mae Hagin	Distinguished Service Award; Arkansas Library Association
1982	Fred K. Darragh	Bessie Moore Trustee Award; Arkansas Library Association
1982	Jo Ann Newell	Bessie Moore Trustee Award; Arkansas Library Association
1984	Bob Razer	LaNell Compton Award; Arkansas Library Association
1988	Fred K. Darragh	Trustee Citation; American Library Association
1988	Leland Gordon	Bessie Moore Trustee Award; Arkansas Library Association
1988	Bob Razer	LaNell Compton Award; Arkansas Library Association
1989	Bobby Roberts	Arkansiana Award; Arkansas Library Association
1993	Bobby Roberts	Distinguished Service Award; Arkansas Library Association
1993	Bob Razer	President's Award; Arkansas Library Association
1994	Bobby Roberts	Presidential Appointment; National Commission on Libraries and Information Science
1995	Tom Dillard	Bessie Moore Trustee Award; Arkansas Library Association
1997	Bobby Roberts	Librarian of the Year; *Library Journal*
1997	Tom Dillard	President's Award; Arkansas Library Association
1997	Timothy Nutt	President's Award; Arkansas Library Association
1999	Bobby Roberts	Presidential Appointment; National Commission on Libraries and Information Science
2000	Dwain Gordon	President's Award; Arkansas Library Association
2001	Jamie Melson	Paraprofessional Award; Arkansas Library Association
2002	Bobby Roberts	Award of Merit; Arkansas Chapter, American Institute of Architects
2004	Bob Razer	LaNell Compton Award; Arkansas Library Association

2007	Bettye Fowler Kerns	Ann Lightsey Children's Librarian Award; Arkansas Library Association
2007	Grif Stockley	Arkansiana Award; Arkansas Library Association
2007	Sarah Ziegenbein	Distinguished Service Award; Arkansas Library Association
2009	Linda Bly	Award of Merit; Quapaw Quarter Association
2009	Bobby Roberts	Jimmy Strawn Historic Preservation Award; Quapaw Quarter Association
2009	Bob Razer	Walter L. Brown Award (*Pulaski County Historical Society Review*); Arkansas Historical Association
2009	Grif Stockley	Best Article (*Pulaski County Historical Society Review*); Arkansas Historical Association
2009	Bob Razer and Kathryn Heller	Best Graphics Award (*Pulaski County Historical Society Review*); Arkansas Historical Association
2009	Bob Razer	Best Biography, Autobiography, or Memoir Award (*Pulaski County Historical Society Review*); Arkansas Historical Association
2009	Shirley Schuette	Best Edited Documents Award (*Pulaski County Historical Society Review*); Arkansas Historical Association
2009	Encyclopedia of Arkansas History & Culture Staff	Diamond Award; Arkansas Historical Association
2009	Grif Stockley	J. G. Ragsdale Book Award; Arkansas Historical Association
2010	Jamie Metrailer	Walter L. Brown Award for Best Article; Arkansas Historical Association
2010	Bob Razer and Kathryn Heller	Walter L. Brown Award for Best Use of Graphics (*Pulaski County Historical Society Review*); Arkansas Historical Association
2010	Bob Razer, Editor	Walter L. Brown Award, Best County or Local Journal (*Pulaski County Historical Society Review*); Arkansas Historical Association
2010	Kay Bland	Lifetime Membership Award; Arkansas Association of Instructional Media
2010	Butler Center for Arkansas Studies	Award of Merit for the Korean War Project; Arkansas Historical Association

Distinguished Lecture Series

The public library has hosted a variety of speakers throughout its history, but this set of endowed lectures took the library's adult programming to a new level.

Fred K. Darragh Jr. Distinguished Lecture
Committed to Civil Liberties and Education

1999	Paul Duke, journalist and former moderator of *Washington Week in Review*, the longest-running news program on PBS, "Politics and the Media"
2000	Georgiann Geyer, foreign correspondent, "A World View on the Eve of the Millennium"
2001	David Rusk, author, speaker, and consultant on urban policy, "Economic and Demographic Development Trends in the Little Rock Metropolitan Area"
2001	Bette Greene, author, "The Craft of Writing Fiction for Children and Adults"
2002	Gayle Seymour, professor of art history at UCA, "Beyond Memorials: Art in Public Places"
2003	Robin Wright, journalist, author, and foreign affairs analyst, "The Middle East & Islam: The Next Challenges"
2004	John Seigenthaler, founder of Freedom Forum First Amendment Center at Vanderbilt University, "James K. Polk: The Unappreciated President"
2005	Carlos Fuentes, novelist and essayist, "An Evening with Carlos Fuentes"
2006	Carl Bernstein, journalist, "Investigative Reporting from Watergate to the Clinton Era to the Bush Era"
2007	Readers' Theater, "Who Will Build Arkansas? A Readers' Theater on Race Relations and Community"
2008	Jill Conner Browne, novelist, "Being the Queen Mother"
2009	Charlaine Harris, novelist

J. N. Heiskell Distinguished Lecture
Committed to Excellence in Journalism

2000	Helen Thomas, former White House correspondent for United Press International
2001	Roy Reed, author and journalist, "The Gazette Years from 1956–1965"
2002	Ernest Dumas, journalist, "Clairvoyants, Fabulists, Eccentrics and Other Characters at the Old Gray Lady"
2003	Taylor Branch, Pulitzer Prize–winning author and national authority on America's civil rights movement, "On Books and Citizenship"
2004	Walter R. Mears, Associated Press reporter and Pulitzer Prize winner, "Deadlines Past"
2005	Jim Hightower, political commentator and author, "Stop Beating around the Bush"
2006	Bruce Bartlett, syndicated newspaper columnist, "Imposter: How George W. Bush Bankrupted America and Betrayed the Reagan Legacy"
2007	Jay Barth, professor of history at Hendrix College, "Aftermath: The Geography of Race and Politics since the 1957 Little Rock Crisis"
2008	David Pryor, former governor and U.S. senator, "Arkansas: The Unique Character of Its Politics and Journalism"
2009	Dexter Filkins, *New York Times* correspondent, "Forever War"

Rabbi Ira E. Sanders Distinguished Lecture
Committed to Intellectual Freedom

2000	Readers' Theater (produced by William B. Jones Jr.)
2001	Michael Lienesch, political science professor at the University of North Carolina, "To Teach or Not To Teach: Reviewing the Impact of the Scopes Monkey Trial"
2002	B. J. Bolden, associate professor of English at Chicago State University and director of the Gwendolyn Brooks Center for Black Literature and Creative Writing, "The Work and Life of Langston Hughes"
2002	Readers' Theater, "God Save This Honorable Court: The 1981 Creation Science Trial"
2003	Knowing Your Past Foundation, "Remembering the Righteous"
2004	Taylor Branch, Pulitzer Prize–winning author and national authority on America's civil rights movement, "Democracy in Black and White: Brown Plus 50 Years"
2005	Alex Kurzem, eyewitness to Nazi atrocities, "The Mascot: The Extraordinary Story of a Young Jewish Boy and an SS Extermination Squad"
2006	Grif Stockley, author, "Ruled by Race: The Historical Context of the 50th Anniversary of the 1957 Little Rock School Desegregation Crisis"
2007	James H. Cone, professor of systematic theology at Union Theological Seminary in New York City, "Little Rock and Arkansas: Their Significance in the Last 50 Years of Civil Rights History"
2008	John Berry, author, "Rising Tides: A Conversation about Man against Man, Man against Nature, and Nature against Man"
2009	Ronald Mallett, professor of physics at the University of Connecticut, "Time Traveler: A Scientist's Personal Mission to Make Time Travel a Reality"

Booker Worthen Prize Winners

Established in 1999, the Booker Worthen Prize is awarded for the best fiction or nonfiction work by an author living in the Pulaski and Perry County areas served by the Central Arkansas Library System.

1999	S. Charles Bolton, *Arkansas, 1800–1860: Remote and Restless*
2000	Mara Leveritt, *The Boys on the Tracks*
2001	Morris S. Arnold, *The Rumble of a Distant Drum: The Quapaws and Old World Newcomers, 1673–1804*
2002	Grif Stockley, *Blood in Their Eyes: The Elaine Race Massacres of 1919*
2003	Mara Leveritt, *Devil's Knot: The True Story of the West Memphis Three*
2004	Kevin Brockmeier, *The Truth about Celia*
2005	Carolyn Earle Billingsley, *Communities of Kinship: Antebellum Families and the Settlement of the Cotton Frontier*
2006	Sidney S. McMath, *Promises Kept*
2007	Kevin Brockmeier, *A Brief History of the Dead*
2008	Elizabeth Jacoway, *Turn Away Thy Son*
2009	Trenton Lee Stewart, *The Mysterious Benedict Society and the Perilous Journey*
2010	Grif Stockley, *Ruled by Race: Black/White Relations in Arkansas from Slavery to the Present*

Collection Development and Circulation Growth

The following chart shows growth in the collection and circulation of materials at the Little Rock Public Library/Central Arkansas Library System. The figures are taken from the annual reports and represent the status on December 31 of each year.

Year	Number of Items	Circulation
1910	5,000	38,570
1915	21,602	102,717
1920	32,858	134,788
1925	37,972	142,317
1930	55,000	273,229
1935	55,919	282,152
1940	74,000	302,333
1945	89,912	218,093
1950	111,084	263,548
1955	129,595	268,791
1960	132,105	278,076
1965	157,619	356,427
1970	200,903	361,512
1975	399,458	699,607
1980	unknown	743,986
1985	unknown	721,897
1990	524,390	945,097
1995	502,537	815,811
2000	613,110	1,212,453
2005	748,486	1,594,358
2009	927,833	2,303,702

Bibliography

Primary Sources

The CALS Collection, MSS 97-01, Butler Center for Arkansas Studies, Arkansas Studies Institute, Little Rock.

Carnegie Corporation of New York Records, Rare Book and Manuscript Library, Columbia University Libraries. Series II.A.1.a, reel 17. A copy of this file is now available as part of the CALS collection.

Vera Snook Papers, University of Illinois at Urbana-Champaign, University Archives, University Library, Graduate School of Information and Library Sciences, Director's Alumni File, RS 18/1/42, Box 28. A copy of this file is now available as part of the CALS collection.

Books

Adams, Thomas, and Ruth V. Gross. *Traveling between Worlds: German-American Encounters.* College Station: Texas A & M University Press, 2006.

Arkansas Gazette Centennial Edition. Little Rock: Gazette Publishing Co., November 20, 1919.

Battles, Matthew. *Library: An Unquiet History.* New York: W. W. Norton & Co., 2003.

Benidt, Bruce Weir. *The Library Book: Centennial History of the Minneapolis Public Library.* Minneapolis, MN: Minneapolis Public Library and Information Center, 1985.

Bobinski, George S. *Carnegie Libraries: Their History and Impact on American Public Library Development.* Chicago, IL: American Library Association, 1969.

Bostwick, Arthur E. *The American Public Library.* New York: D. Appleton and Company, 1910.

Carmichael, James V., Jr. "Southerners in the North and Northerners in the South; The Impact of the Library School of the University of Illinois on Southern Librarianship." In *Women's Work: Vision and Change in Librarianship.* Urbana, IL: Graduate School of Library and Information Science, 1994.

Carnegie, Andrew. *The Autobiography of Andrew Carnegie.* Boston and New York: Houghton Mifflin Co., 1920.

Dain, Phyllis. *The New York Public Library: A History of Its Founding and Early Years.* New York: The New York Public Library, Astor, Lenox and Tilden Foundations, 1972.

Ditzion, Sidney Herbert. *Arsenals of a Democratic Culture: A Social History of the American Public Library Movement in New England and the Middle States from 1850 to 1900.* Chicago, IL: American Library Association, 1947.

Eaton, Thelma, ed. *Contributions to American Library History.* Champaign, IL: The Illini Union Bookstore, 1961.

Fersh, George and Mildred. *Bessie Moore, A Biography.* Little Rock, AR: August House, 1986.

Garrison, Dee. *Apostles of Culture: The Public Librarian and American Society, 1876–1920.* New York: The Free Press, Inc., 1979.

Gleason, Eliza Atkins. *The Southern Negro and the Public Library: A Study of the Government and Administration of Public Library Service to Negroes in the South.* Chicago, IL: University of Chicago Press, 1941.

Harris, Michael H. *A Guide to Research in American Library History,* 2nd edition. Metuchen, NJ: The Scarecrow Press, Inc., 1974.

Herndon, Dallas T. *Centennial History of Arkansas.* Chicago, IL: The S. J. Clarke Publishing Company, 1922.

Hill, A. B., ed. *Four Years with the Public Schools in Arkansas, 1923–1927.* Little Rock: State Department of Education, printed by Calvert-McBride Printing, Fort Smith, 1927.

Joeckel, Carlton Bruns. *The Government of the American Public Library.* Chicago, IL: University of Chicago Press, 1935.

Johnson, Alvin. *Pioneer's Progress: An Autobiography.* New York: The Viking Press, 1952.

Jones, Reinette F. *Library Service to African Americans in Kentucky, from the Reconstruction Era to the 1960s.* Jefferson, NC: McFarland & Company, Inc., Publishers, 2002.

Kaser, David. *A Book for Sixpence: The Circulating Library in America.* Pittsburgh, PA: Beta Phi Mu, 1980.

Kranich, Nancy, ed. *Libraries & Democracy: The Cornerstones of Liberty.* Chicago, IL: American Library Association, 2001.

Lee, Robert Ellis. *Continuing Education for Adults through the American Public Library, 1833–1964.* Chicago, IL: American Library Association, 1966.

Leigh, Robert D. *The Public Library in the United States.* New York: Columbia University, 1950.

Roy, F. Hampton, Sr., Charles Witsell Jr., and Cheryl Griffith Nichols. *How We Lived: Little Rock as an American City.* Little Rock: August House, 1984.

Shera, Jesse H. *Foundations of the Public Library: The Origins of the Public Library Movement in New England 1629–1855.* Hamden, CT: The Shoe String Press, 1974 (originally University of Chicago Press, 1947).

Thomison, Dennis. *A History of the American Library Association 1876–1972.* Chicago, IL: American Library Association, 1978.

United States Bureau of Education; University of Wisconsin Digital Collections Center. *Public Libraries in the United States of America; Their History, Condition, and Management. Special Report, Department of the Interior, Bureau of Education. Part I.* Washington DC: Government Printing Office, 1876. Online at http://digital.library.wisc.edu/1711.dl/History.PublicLibs.

Yust, William F. *Library Legislation*, reprint of *Manual of Library Economy (1911), Chapter IX,* Chicago, IL: American Library Association Publishing Board, 1921.

Online Sources

Banks, Dean. *Arkansas Diamonds: Dreams, Myths, and Reality*, www.pcahs.com.

Encyclopedia of Arkansas History & Culture, www.encyclopediaofarkansas.net.

Gates Foundation. *98 Annual Reports for the William H. Gates Foundation and the Gates Library Foundation*, http://www.gatesfoundation.org.

"Information about the Library: History," Niedersaechische Staats - und Universitaetsbibliothek Goettingen, http://elib.sub.uni-goettingen.de/ebene_1/1_geschichte.htm.en.

Mausolf, Lisa B., and Elizabeth Durfee Hengen. "Edward Lippincott Tilton: A Monograph on His Architectural Practice." Currier Museum of Art, 2007, http://www.nh.gov/nhdhr/publications/documents/etilton_monograph.pdf.

Smith, Sandra Taylor, and Anne Wagner Speed. *Little Rock's Capitol View Neighborhood Historic District.* Little Rock: Arkansas Preservation Program, www.arkansaspreservation.org/pdf/publications/Capitol_View.pdf.

Sturges, Paul. "The Public Library and Reading by the Masses: Historical Perspectives on the USA and Britain 1850–1900," 60th IFLA General Conference, Conference Proceedings, August 21–27, 1994, http://www.ifla.org/IV/ifla60/60-stup.htm.

Articles

Arkansas Free Library Service Bureau, State Department of Education. "Report to the Julius Rosenwald Fund for the Years November 1, 1929 to October 31, 1931." (1932).

Berry, John N., III. "Bobby Roberts: *LJ* Librarian of the Year 1997." *Library Journal* 123 (January 1998): 44–46.

Carmichael, James V., Jr. "Southern Librarianship and the Culture of Resentment." *Libraries & Culture* 40 (Summer 2005).

Croteau, Jeffrey. "Yet More American Circulating Libraries: A Preliminary Checklist of Brooklyn (New York) Circulating Libraries." *Library History* 22 (November 2006): 171–180.

Fultz, Michael. "Black Public Libraries in the South in the Era of De Jure Segregation." *Libraries & the Cultural Record* 41 (Summer 2006).

Holley, Edward G., and Robert F. Schremser. *The Library Services and Construction Act: An Historical Overview from the Viewpoint of Major Participants* 18 (1983).

Johnson, William. "Leaders in Many Communities Labor Heroically for Libraries." *Arkansas Democrat*, June 2, 1935.

Levinson, Nancy Smiler. "Taking It to the Streets: The History of the Book Wagon." *Library Journal* (May 1991).

Luyt, Brendan. "The ALA, Public Libraries and the Great Depression." *Library History* 23 (June 2007).

Martin, Rosemary. "Public Librarians as Employers: Expectations." *Journal of Library Administration* 11, 3–4 (1990): 175–186.

Meyer, Dr. Hans Joachim. "Dresden: Treasures from the Saxon State Library, Remarks at the Opening of the Exhibition, April 10, 1996," online at http://www.loc.gov/exhibits/dres/dresrema.html.

Moses, James L. "The Law of Life is the Law of Service": Rabbi Ira Sanders and the Quest for Racial and Social Justice in Arkansas, 1926–1963. *Southern Jewish History: Journal of the Southern Jewish Historical Society* 10 (2007).

Razer, Bob. "A Chapter in Arkansas Library History: A History of the Arkansas Library Association." *Arkansas Libraries* 43 (December 1986): 6–15.

———. "The Library, YES! The 1992 Amendment 3 Campaign." *Arkansas Libraries* 50 (April 1993): 5–14.

Roberts, Bobby. "Arkansas Library Association." *Encyclopedia of Library Information Science 13th Edition*, pp. 31–36.

Ross, Frances Mitchell. "The New Woman as Club Woman and Social Activist in Turn of the Century Arkansas." *Arkansas Historical Quarterly* 50 (Winter 1991): 317–351.

Sowder, Leta, Allie Beth Martin, and Lelia Heasley. "Work of the State Library Commission 1937–1947." *Arkansas Historical Quarterly* 6 (Winter 1947): 450–457.

Stanick, Katherine. "Symbiotic Organizations." *Arkansas Libraries* 34 (March 1977): 2–4.

Story, Kenneth. "Arkansas Listings in the National Register of Historic Places." *Arkansas Historical Quarterly* 59 (Autumn 2000): 318–321.

Taylor, David. "Ladies of the Club: An Arkansas Story." *Wilson Library Bulletin* 59 (January 1985): 324–327.

van Slyck, Abigail A. "'The Utmost Amount of Effictiv [*sic*] Accommodation': Andrew Carnegie and the Reform of the American Library." *The Journal of the Society of Architectural Historians* 50 (December 1991): 359–383.

Woodruff, Jane Georgine. "William E. Woodruff as Remembered by His Three Daughters." *Arkansas Gazette Centennial Edition*. Little Rock: Gazette Publishing Co., November 20, 1919.

Published Reports

Himmel & Wilson, Library Consultants. *Inventing the Future of Library Service in Arkansas.* Little Rock: The Library, 1999.

Kwendeche, "Determination of Eligibility, Application, submitted to the Department of Arkansas Heritage—Arkansas Historic Preservation Program, August 2005," W. G. Hall—Anthony Building, 1601 Dr. Martin Luther King, Jr. Drive (Formerly High Street), Little Rock, AR, 72202.

Schallhorn, Susan K. *Final Report: The Governor's Conference on Library and Information Services.* Little Rock: Arkansas State Library, 1992.

Schenk, Gretchen Knief. *Survey of the Arkansas Library Commission and the Public Libraries of Arkansas.* Summerville, AL: 1964.

United Community Funds and Councils of America. *The Little Rock Survey: A Four Weeks Study of Public and Private Social Work in Greater Little Rock, Arkansas, April 1939, by the Association of Community Chests and Councils, Inc.* New York: Association of Community Chests and Councils, 1939.

Writers' Program of the Work Projects Administration in the State of Arkansas. *Survey of Negroes in Little Rock and North Little Rock, compiled by the Writers' Program of the Work Projects Administration in the State of Arkansas.* Little Rock: The Urban League of Greater Little Rock, 1941.

Theses and Dissertations

Bayless, Stephanie M. "A Southern Paradox: The Social Activism of Adolphine Fletcher Terry." MA thesis, University of Arkansas at Little Rock, 2008.

Dwellingham, June H. "A General Survey of the Little Rock (Arkansas) Public Library." MLS thesis, Philadelphia: The Drexel Institute of Technology School of Library Science, 1954.

Gates, Jean Kay. "Library Progress in Tax-supported Institutions in Arkansas, 1924–1949." Master's thesis, Catholic University of America, Washington DC, 1951.

Martin, Marilyn. "From Altruism to Activism: The Contributions of Women's Organizations to Arkansas Public Libraries. PhD diss., Denton: Texas Woman's University, 1993.

McNeil, Gladys. "History of the Library in Arkansas." Master's thesis, Oxford: University of Mississippi, 1957.

Tillman, Rosebud Harris. "The History of Public Library Service to Negroes in Little Rock, Arkansas, 1917–1951." MLS thesis, Atlanta, GA: School of Library Service, 1953.

Interviews

Bly, Linda, interview by Nathania Sawyer, June 23, 2010.

Bonner, Melrita Russ, interview by Jajuan Johnson, May 27, 2009.

Brooks, Michael, interview by Nathania Sawyer, June 28, 2010.

Chilcoat, Jennifer, interview by Nathania Sawyer, June 29, 2010.

Coffey, Carol, interview by Nathania Sawyer, June 22, 2010.

Crymes, Alysanne, interview by Nathania Sawyer, June 24, 2010.

Jackson, Melinda, interview by Nathania Sawyer, June 29, 2010.

Jones, Phillip, interview by Nathania Sawyer, June 29, 2010.

Kerns, Bettye, interview by Nathania Sawyer, June 28, 2010.

Melson, Jamie, interview by Nathania Sawyer, June 23, 2010.

Razer, Bob, interview by Nathania Sawyer, June 25, 2010.

Roberts, Bobby, interview by Nathania Sawyer, June 22, 2010.

Smith, Almeta, interview by Jajuan Johnson, May 28, 2009.

Smith, Almeta, interview by Nathania Sawyer, June 25, 2010.

Thompson, Larrie, interview by Nathania Sawyer, June 21, 2010.

Thwing, Valerie, interview by Nathania Sawyer, June 25, 2010.

Yates, Margaret, interview by Nathania Sawyer, June 24, 2010.

From Carnegie to Cyberspace: 100 Years at the Central Arkansas Library System